THE TEACHER TODAY

Tasks, Conditions, Policies

ORGANISATION FOR ECONOMIC CO-OPERATION AND DEVELOPMENT

Pursuant to article 1 of the Convention signed in Paris on 14th December 1960, and which came into force on 30th September 1961, the Organisation for Economic Co-operation and Development (OECD) shall promote policies designed:

- to achieve the highest sustainable economic growth and employment and a rising standard of living in Member countries, while maintaining financial stability, and thus to contribute to the development of the world economy;
- to contribute to sound economic expansion in Member as well as non-member countries in the process of economic development; and
- to contribute to the expansion of world trade on a multilateral, non-discriminatory basis in accordance with international obligations.

The original Member countries of the OECD are Austria, Belgium, Canada, Denmark, France, the Federal Republic of Germany, Greece, Iceland, Ireland, Italy, Luxembourg, the Netherlands, Norway, Portugal, Spain, Sweden, Switzerland, Turkey, the United Kingdom and the United States. The following countries became Members subsequently through accession at the dates indicated hereafter: Japan (28th April 1964), Finland (28th January 1969), Australia (7th June 1971) and New Zealand (29th May 1973).

The Socialist Federal Republic of Yugoslavia takes part in some of the work of the OECD (agreement of 28th October 1961).

Publié en français sous le titre :

L'ENSEIGNANT AUJOURD'HUI
FONCTIONS, STATUT, POLITIQUES

Since the OECD Ministers of Education last met in November 1984, a substantial portion of the work of the Education Committee has addressed policies and practices contributing to the quality of education. As part of that, a study programme was established specifically concerned with teachers and teaching, guided by the Committee's Working Party on "The Condition of Teaching" which met four times between 1986 and 1989. This publication is the general report resulting from that work.

While the aim of improving quality is an important consideration running through this review of the situation of, and policies towards, teachers, the brief for the study was set widely to encompass the variety of factors and developments of relevance to the formulation of those policies. To maintain manageable scope, teachers in post-secondary education and training have been excluded from direct consideration. The work was designed to be complementary to, rather than overlap with, studies on teachers and their working conditions being conducted by other international organisations. Similarly, it complements a parallel CERI enquiry on teacher education and training.

In preparing this report, the Secretariat drew heavily on statements describing recent policies and developments in Member countries submitted by national authorities, as well as on the results of a series of meetings of country representatives and experts. Within the Secretariat, the author of the report is David Istance of the Education and Training Division in the Directorate for Social Affairs, Manpower, and Education. The discussion of the research on teaching contained in Chapter 4 is abridged from a review prepared by Marshall S. Smith and Jennifer O'Day, Dean and Senior Researcher respectively in the School of Education, Stanford University, California.

The report is published on the responsibility of the Secretary-General.

3

CONTENTS

Chapter 6

The Teacher Today: An Overview of the Problem 111

LIST OF TABLES

Chapter 1

TEACHERS – A CENTRAL POLICY CONCERN

THE SPOTLIGHT ON TEACHERS

In the large majority of OECD countries, the condition of teaching is now a matter of intense public concern. The reasons for this, as always in accounting for major developments in education, are manifold and interlocking – no one factor is paramount. What is apparent is that a number of outstanding but diverse factors and concerns have coincided to push the teaching profession squarely under the spotlight of educational debate and policy.

At least four major factors stand out. There is a sense of profound *dissatisfaction* within the teaching body in many countries and the experience during the 1980s of a sharp deterioration in industrial relations between teachers and their employing authorities in some. Teachers feel acutely the pressing demand for *accountability* and the subjection of public services, including education, to the intense glare of outside scrutiny, and this is in turn related to the sheer scale of the resources needed to maintain the teaching force in OECD countries. The emergence of the pursuit of *quality* as a general priority of educational policy has been a hallmark of recent years and with that has come the growing perception of the key role of teachers, both positive and negative, in realising that broad ambition[1]. Finally, there are growing expressions of concern in a number of countries that, following an era of managing a decline of student enrolments and a general surplus of teaching resources, problems of adequate teacher *supply* are re-emerging, especially in key subjects of the curriculum.

This list is not exhaustive. Naturally, other factors too play a role. Nor are all reasons for the prominence teachers now receive equally relevant in all national settings. There are some OECD countries where the standing of the teaching profession has remained relatively high throughout the post-war period. There are some where, whatever the concern about insufficient present or future supply in other systems, teacher unemployment is still the dominant fact (Germany and Ireland represent two examples here, as discussed in Chapter 3 below). Yet despite such differences, in few countries has the question of the standing, competence, and motivation of their teaching forces remained on the sidelines of public discussion. Arguably, any one of the factors listed above would have been sufficient to account for a new prominence. Together, they are a potent mixture indeed.

7

TEACHERS, TEACHING, AND EDUCATION

Underlying presuppositions about teachers and teaching

This report aims to present some of the principal policy issues and relevant international evidence concerning teachers and teaching today. Two points of clarification are necessary at the outset.

First, the report is concerned both with *teachers,* as the professional body charged with actually imparting education, and with *teaching* as the process by which they achieve this. The underlying assumption is that a focus on both is essential. To isolate sharply one from the other is likely either to result in the loss from sight of the ultimate aim of all policy and practice in this field – the provision of a worthwhile, high quality education for all – or it can lead to the neglect of the principal means through which good teaching is to be achieved, namely the teachers themselves. Chapters 2 and 3 focus particularly on the teaching body and its characteristics, while Chapter 4 looks more closely at the teaching process, and Chapter 5 examines the new tasks and challenges confronting teachers and teaching.

Second, reference is freely made throughout this report to the term "the teaching profession" despite the fact that explicit discussion of professions and professionalism is only taken up at the beginning of Chapter 3 and recognising the long-standing discussion about whether teachers do, in fact, constitute a profession. One argument from Chapter 3 can be anticipated at this point to assert that the purely definitional exercise that takes for granted that there is a clear meaning of "professional" as a litmus against which the characteristics of teachers can be compared to test for its presence, that teachers constitute a homogeneous occupational group to be considered together in this regard, and that these two hold up equally across national boundaries, is a largely sterile one. Without begging the question, the term "profession" is deployed in this report as a reflection of normal educational parlance. (It should also be noted that while the issues of status and conditions apply across national boundaries, the terms "profession" and "professional" do not readily translate beyond the English language and hence the debate in some countries about their meaning is culturally specific).

Yet it would be equally misleading to take the opposite stance to maintain that the professional standing of teachers is unproblematic – their own complaints about status and working conditions alone, quite apart from other opinions and developments, are evidence that this is an area fraught with tension. That tension is played out between the triangular forces of the professional *competence and commitment* of teachers (what might be described as "professionalism"), on one side, the professional *demands* which good teaching today exert, on another side, and the professional *recognition* that teachers receive for their efforts in return, on the third. The interplay between this triad surfaces repeatedly throughout this report.

Education and teaching

To highlight the interplay between professional demands, competence, and recognition is to draw attention explicitly to the inter-connectedness between different aspects of teaching policies. Policies directed inordinately at only one or two of these to the neglect of the other(s) will have profound repercussions for the success of those policies. This is both a fundamental premise and a main conclusion of this report. Successful policies for teachers and teaching cannot be developed in isolation from more general educational policies. Accommodating broad visions may not, however, prove comfortable for any of the parties involved. For the policy-making authorities, it demands a more imaginative and less bureaucratic approach than when teaching policies are developed as a set of isolated arrangements each with its own values and traditions. For teacher training establishments, the broad view implies their continual involvement in new developments rather than reliance on tried and established programmes. For teachers themselves, the legitimacy of relating the different aspects of their professional life – training, retraining, individual performance and collective results, professional rewards and career opportunities – may sit uneasily with long practice treating these as separate domains. The adoption of broad perspectives that comprehend the interplay and interconnection of factors and forces is always likely to prove problematic for the traditionalists in education, from whatever side – policy-makers, parents and the community, teachers – they belong.

The importance of the close interrelation between different aspects of teaching and teacher policies extends much further, however, to include the interplay between teaching specifically and education more widely. (We signal again that the levels of education systems directly referred to in this report do not include higher and adult education). The common perception of problematic status, for instance, is only partially about teachers *per se* as an occupational group with that status shaped by a particular set of labour market and sociological forces. Teachers' status is also fundamentally shaped by the general standing of education as a whole. The generally poor public perception of education and the spirit of pessimism that took hold in many quarters in the 1970s was probably as responsible as any other single factor for the feeling of malaise that affected teachers specifically. Equally, policy efforts to raise the attractiveness of teaching in general, or of the profession in specific sectors such as primary or vocational education, will need to adopt as their ambition as much the improvement of the provision and the status of that education as of the rights and benefits of the professional body concerned, if they are to succeed. In concrete terms this means, for example, that specific campaigns to meet problems of teacher supply through advertising the availability of career openings in a profession with an attractive image will lose much of their impact if the general tenor of public and official attitudes towards the education service is not equally positive.

This interplay between general educational and specific teaching policies is nowhere more clearly illustrated than in the importance now accorded in many OECD countries to the pursuit of quality. It has taken time since the difficulties and pessimism of the 1970s and early 1980s for the perception to be widely shared that the success of educational reforms, no matter how well they are conceived in principle, will be only fortuitous if the teachers who are actually responsible are not made an explicit and pivotal plank of those reforms. An uncommitted and poorly motivated teaching body will have disastrous results for even the best intentions for improvement. Teachers lie at the heart of the educational process. The greater the importance attached to education as a whole – whether for cultural transmission, for social cohesion and justice, or for the human resource development so critical in modern, technology-based economies[2] – the higher is the priority that must be accorded to the teachers responsible for that education.

Much emphasis has thus been given in recent years to the key contribution teachers make to the pursuit of quality in education. Without competent and motivated teachers, aspirations for a high quality education service are likely to founder. A joint Italy/OECD conference held in Rome in May 1986 encapsulated this in its title "Quality in Education: The Vital Role of Teachers". That is the positive side of the equation. But the opposite conclusion cannot be drawn – that teachers are to blame if and when disappointments arise about educational performance or the speed of change. Teachers are the necessary, indeed the most necessary, ingredients of quality but still not sufficient to guarantee it. They should be given, and should accept, a large measure of responsibility but they cannot be held solely accountable. Their contribution must be understood in terms of the curricular, organisational, and social context in which they work. It needs to be prefaced too by the understanding that that contribution depends upon the establishment of conditions conducive to sustained high levels of morale and motivation and the full exercise of professional development.

How far the full ramification of the fundamental chain of causation – a healthy society and economy *means* a well-functioning education system *means* an active, motivated, and highly competent teaching force – has been grasped by all, is still an open question. The key role of a highly skilled and well motivated teaching force has certainly been accorded in principle as illustrated, for example, by the conclusions issued by the OECD Ministers of Education concerning teacher policies when they last met in 1984[3]. But no matter how obvious that contribution may appear when stated, it has been too often neglected. In this decade, the reform movement in the United States can be divided into different waves, as described by Wagner in an OECD-commissioned study, precisely in terms of the recognition accorded to teachers. He distinguishes the "first wave" from the "second wave" of reforms through the more concrete and sensitive approach to the actual realities of implementing change, especially through the teachers themselves who are at the front line:

> "With the objectives of educational reform generally accepted, a 'second wave' of reports have offered more specific recommendations for achieving the desired outcomes. These reports, including the Carnegie Forum's *A Nation Prepared* and the National Governor's Association's *Time for Results*, took as their starting points two apparent barriers to improvements in educational quality and student learning. First, schools appear to be entering a period when the growing demand for new teachers will not be met from the traditional source of new teacher graduates. Thus, the reports devote considerable attention to ways to ensure adequate supplies of able, qualified teachers. And, second, in probing more deeply into how changes might improve schooling, the panels recognised the contradiction in seeking to attract able, talented individuals to teach in an environment that hardly promotes initiative and creativity (and learning)"[4].

Moving beyond statements of good intent and analysis, whether prepared by politicians, officials, interest groups and expert bodies, or teachers, is, however, another matter. The critical insight about the key role of teachers must enter into everyday practice and thinking. To achieve that is a major challenge for the decade ahead.

THE POLITICAL CONTEXT

The need for consensus

Responding to that challenge implies the establishment of a broad measure of consensus. This in turn implies widespread agreement on two matters: first, that teaching is a vital and highly demanding job that merits corresponding recognition and reward, both pecuniary and non pecuniary; second, that the highest standards of professional performance and commitment are to be expected from all teachers in return. The cycles here may turn out to be either vicious or virtuous. A groundswell of optimism and public recognition for the difficult and demanding task that teachers perform can reap ready rewards in the form of boosted morale, enhanced motivation, and the greater attractiveness of the profession that can become self-generating, with obviously positive results for teaching and learning. Distrust, confrontation, and mutual suspicion between the different parties involved can only result ultimately in dented morale and a decline of teaching standards. That is a vicious circle that modern societies and economies can ill afford.

Emerging from the 1980s, which witnessed damaging industrial disputes by teachers over pay and conditions in countries and locations as diverse as Greece, Italy and Spain, Ireland and the United Kingdom, Sweden and Norway, New Zealand, and certain of the major cities and districts of the United States, to seek the establishment of a virtuous, rather than vicious, circle may appear a forlorn hope. In fact, it is nearer the truth to assert that countries confront little choice about setting a positive process of enhanced recognition, motivation, and professionalism in train. Not only is it implied by the ever-growing requirements of a high quality education service and the emerging new tasks and challenges of today (as discussed in the latter chapters of this report) but also by the need to meet the gradually looming question of a potential crisis of teacher supply that can only be permanently averted by strenuous efforts to make the teaching profession a genuinely attractive one (Chapter 3). It would be a tragically retrograde step if the dominant issue of the 1990s ceased to be a continuation of the concern of the eighties to ensure *qualitative* improvement of the teaching force and heralded instead a return to the overwhelming *quantitative* planning problem of the 1960s of how to fill vacant posts.

It is impossible to prescribe in the abstract ideal mechanisms for negotiation on policies and conditions that might foster and maintain consensus. The role of teacher unions and associations varies widely cross-nationally and a number of countries have recently experienced important changes in terms of the centralisation/decentralisation of decision-making that intimately affect the locus of teachers' negotiations. It is possible to assert, however, that those management and decision-making structures should be scrutinised to ascertain how far they promote the involvement of all the "actors" concerned and the active pursuit of a spirit of consensus.

Recognising the new political context

One condition for the establishment of a new consensus is that teachers and their representatives, as well as other players in the process, come to terms with the fact that the political context in which they work, characterised by greater public interest in educational results and in participation in the decision-making process, has altered irrevocably over the past two or three decades. Accepting this does not imply that all demands for greater accountability are justified in whatever form. Rigidly bureaucratic top-down forms of accountability that claim to promote professionalism may well actually undermine the necessary exercise of professional judgement, serving neither teachers nor students well. Yet on the other side, arguments for enhanced professional status are frequently couched in references to bygone years in terms that are simply not realistic. Too often, romantic references are made to a highly selective version of the past, neglecting the degree to which teachers in the early decades of this century were poorly paid, insecurely employed (especially if female), and pursuing careers that exploited moderate skills and allowed only minimal professional development. Too often, a false equation is made between professional autonomy, on the one hand, and freedom from any external contact and accountability, on the other.

Coming to terms with the changed political environment means recognition of at least three new conditions. First, parents are more highly educated and articulate than ever before[5]. One result of this is that their expectations for their children's education are higher than ever; the social mechanisms for limiting parental ambition are increasingly as unaccepted as they are unacceptable. Extensive parental experience of the education system through their own schooling also precludes a return to the closed world of the school room where the teacher's word went unchallenged (the less positive side of the higher social status that *some* teachers, especially principals, enjoyed in years past).

Second, community involvement in education is taking forms that necessarily impinge on the activities of individual teachers in classrooms, workshops, and staffrooms. For instance, there are increasing efforts to improve the links and contacts between the world of education and that of employment, whether they take the form of the greater exchange of information between the two, or of programmes located in both settings, or of the establishment of curricula and qualifications that depend on the substantial involvement of employers. Indeed, teachers are increasingly expected to be the active promoters of such contacts. Another relevant example of community involvement in education is the more prominent role of interest groups in education at the national, regional, and local levels, each with articulate (and sometimes conflicting) claims concerning the organisation and contents of learning.

Third, a general policy feature of many OECD countries is the growing demand for efficiency in the use and management of resources, especially public resources, as a condition of their expenditure. Once again, that demand may not always take forms that arguably are in the best interests of education, nor even of their most efficient use. Yet whether that demand is for more regular evaluations of schools and colleges and the work teachers do, or a greater willingness on the part of educational institutions to open their doors to the outside world, or the more formalised step of developing performance indicators[6], it is unlikely to be short-lived. And the dangers of simplistic, distorting forms of evaluation and appraisal will be significantly reduced if teachers themselves are actively involved in their construction and implementation. Indeed, that is a precondition of their success.

The need for comprehensive analyses and the frank exchange of views

If one major condition for forging a new consensus is the positive acceptance of a changed political climate and context, another is the need for all parties involved in educational decision-making, including policy-makers, officials, and teachers, to support the honest exchange of ideas and viewpoints. Where confrontation and distrust between teachers and their employing authorities are the order of the day, political considerations come to distort that exchange. It would be wholly unrealistic to expect the politically-charged nature of educational debate to evaporate entirely. The point is instead that a predominant atmosphere of politicisation and confrontation represents a substantial hurdle to educational improvement and to the open discussion of solutions to outstanding problems.

Examples of the limits to forthright analysis help illustrate how certain important issues may be kept off political agendas. How infrequent it is for teachers to admit publicly that some of their colleagues are ill-suited to the profession, through fear of undermining solidarity and of exposure to the charge that incompetence is commonplace. Yet teachers' private conversation is replete with adverse comments about certain of their colleagues. Scarcely less common is it for those in positions of political authority to state unequivocally that teaching well done is an arduous and totally demanding occupation fully warranting substantial reward or that serious problems of future supply of teachers are foreseeable, in each case because of the political pressure to make the profession more attractive that would inevitably follow. But in so doing, the scope for long-term and gradual solutions is reduced and may even be jeopardized. How difficult it has often proved for teachers' representatives to admit the problems of indiscipline and difficulties of control in many school classrooms, through concern that that admittance would either undermine claims for professional respect or that it might be construed as blaming individual students for systemic deficiencies. Yet without a common perception of the problem, it is the teacher herself or himself who is then left to cope with the highly stressful, sometimes distressing, consequences.

*

*   *

To reiterate, it can scarcely be expected that a matter of such vital national concern as education and one which is such an important source of employment (the next chapter gives quantitative indications of teacher numbers) should be devoid of political content. That very importance, however, argues powerfully for the honest and forthright exchange of information and viewpoints whenever possible. The aim of this report is to contribute to that exchange drawing on international evidence and experience.

13

NOTES AND REFERENCES

1. A summary of recent OECD work on quality in education is contained in OECD (1989), *Schools and Quality: An International Report*, Paris. The particular role of teachers in realising high quality education was the subject of a special international conference jointly organised by the Italian national authorities and the OECD and held in Rome in May 1986: "Quality in Education: The Vital Role of Teachers".

2. Amply discussed in OECD (1989), *Education and the Economy in a Changing Society*, Paris, which is a compilation of the documentation for, and conclusions of, an Intergovernmental Conference of that title held in Paris in March 1988.

3. OECD (1985), "OECD Ministers Discuss Education in Modern Society", Paris (Document on General Distribution) pp. 44-48.

4. Wagner, A. (1987), "Social and Economic Aspects of Teaching: The Attractivenes of the Profession" (OECD working document) pp. 2-4. As Wagner reports in his paper, the "second wave" reform reports include: Carnegie Forum on Education and the Economy, Task Force on Teaching as a Profession, *A Nation Prepared: Teachers for the 21st Century*, 1986; National Governors' Association, *Time for Results: The Governors' 1991 Report on Education*, 1986; California Commission on the Teaching Profession, *Who Will Teach Our Children? A Strategy for Improving California's Schools*, 1985; American Federation of Teachers, Task Force on the Future of Education, *The Revolution that is Overdue: Looking Toward the Future of Teaching and Learning*, 1986; The Holmes Group, Tomorrow's Teachers, 1986; Committee for Economic Development, *Investing in Our Children: Business and the Public Schools*, 1986.

5. The OECD education statistics data bank contains information on the education and training received by pupils and students in the mainstream system, as well as on teachers and expenditures for that provision, not on general attainment levels of adults (and parents) after they have left. That latter subject has been investigated through a separate enquiry on "The Educational Attainment of the Labour Force", published as Chapter 2 of OECD (1989), *Employment Outlook*, Paris.

6. A substantial international project on educational indicators has begun in OECD's CERI with initial conferences jointly organised by the OECD and the United States in Washington D.C. held in November 1987, and by the OECD and France in Poitiers in March 1988.

Chapter 2

TEACHERS IN OECD COUNTRIES: SOME BASIC FACTS AND ISSUES

INTRODUCTION: DIVERSITY OF SOURCES AND DEFINITIONS

This chapter aims to provide an overview of a certain number of key facts and developments concerning teachers in OECD countries. This is not a comprehensive review. The enquiry into the "Condition of Teaching" on which this report is based never held the descriptive documentation of facts and arrangements as its primary purpose, particularly as such documentation is or has been the explicit object of other recent international enquiries[1]. In addition, developments on complex matters such as teacher status or supply require specific analysis and interpretation rather than broad-brush description, and thus are taken up instead in subsequent chapters. The purpose here is to establish an empirical introduction and foundation for the report through consideration of a number of key facts as well as some of the general issues they raise.

The statistics deployed below are drawn from a variety of sources – the OECD's own education and labour force data bank, country reports written expressly for the OECD activity on the Condition of Teaching from which this report emanates, other published national material. This imposes substantial limits on the comparability of the data and precludes precise comparisons of actual magnitudes. The figures presented should instead be viewed as indicative of trends and global developments.

There is, in fact, no single established source of international statistics on teachers across the range of topics covered in this report. The OECD's own education data bank has been substantially revised in line with accords drawn up by the relevant branches of this Organisation, the EEC, and UNESCO so limiting the possibilities for calculating series prior to 1984 (the first year of the new questionnaires). Whatever the year in question, the value and comparability of the data are still critically dependent on the definitions, coverage, and quality of the information sent by the countries from which the base is constructed. Countries differ concerning the degree to which their teacher data include various non-teaching and administrative personnel, the types and sectors of education and training that are counted in and to which teaching staff refers, and the definitions and statistical treatment of full-time and part-time teachers.

There is a popular misconception that these differences between countries are sufficiently minor, especially as teacher data are so fundamental an element of the body of education statistics, that the calculation of indicators such as pupil/teacher ratios across countries should prove to be a relatively routine, technical matter. Closer scrutiny reveals, however, just how complex even this exercise turns out to be[2]. That said, it should be emphasized that improvements to the aforementioned data bases have been made over the past several years. And the current thirst for international information and indicators suggest that still further improvements in terms of the coverage and comparability of statistics on teachers would be widely welcomed. For that to be achieved, however, sustained efforts will be needed to make good the current lack.

THE SIZE OF THE TEACHING FORCE

Continuing the definitional theme, it is clear that the final estimate for the total numbers of teachers employed in any given country depends critically on the width of the definition of "teacher" and on whether individuals are counted, or full-time equivalents calculated. Should pre-primary staff be included when in some countries (such as the Netherlands) this sector is fully integrated into the school system whereas in others (such as Finland) they are not actually considered to be teachers?[3] Where should the cut-off be drawn at the upper stages of secondary and tertiary education and extending how far outside the formal school and college system to include teachers and trainers in non-formal and informal programmes? To these questions, even the country replies to the OECD/UNESCO/SOEC questionnaires differ significantly. Yet, Table 1 can usefully make at least one simple, telling point: there are very substantial numbers indeed of people employed by education systems as teachers. Though the gaps and varying coverage in Table 1 do not permit a strict ratio to be calculated, teachers clearly comprise a significant proportion of the labour force (compare with magnitudes of the latter displayed in Table 5).

That point, however obvious, is of particular relevance to certain of the questions discussed in the next two chapters – namely, professional status and rewards, and the key role of teachers in improving educational quality. The sheer volume of numbers of teachers has a clear impact on the pursuit of professional status if the aspiration is to enjoy comparable privileges to those already gained by prestigious occupational groups such as doctors and lawyers. It has also profound budgetary implications for efforts to raise rewards across-the-board in order to increase the attractiveness of teaching as an occupation. Concerning quality, the quantitative dimensions of the task of raising and maintaining professional skills and knowledge through such mechanisms as in-service training (INSET) or detailed teacher appraisal for all are given approximate scale through consideration of the sheer numbers involved. Numbers rarely settle the matter on any of these questions but they are a significant factor.

Even a rapid examination of Table 1 provides convincing illustrations of the methodological caveats emphasized in the preceding section concerning the differences in country coverage of their statistics on teachers and the difficulty of putting together a comprehensive set of figures for all countries. Even for such basic information as the total number of teachers employed in a single recent year across OECD countries broken down by level of education, this is not readily available, as the gaps and differences show; still less is comparability across the entire OECD family of countries assured.

Table 1
TOTAL NUMBERS OF TEACHERS IN OECD COUNTRIES BY LEVEL
1986/87

Country	Pre-primary	First level	Second-level/first stage	Second level/second stage: general	Second level/second stage: technical and vocational[a]	Special education
Australia[h]	8 563	90 685	..	101 115	..	4 921
Austria	..	33 100	54 934	19 085	18 313	..
Belgium	..	68 420[c]	..	103 999[d]	..	..
Canada	..	180 476[c]	..	121 301	..	..
Denmark	3 675	34 376	31 414	7 578[f]	..	14 297
France	73 192[g]	239 438[h]	182 366	89 807[g]	56 756[g]	44 644
Germany	5 311	131 351	276 348	73 591	53 031	934
Greece[i]	7 617	37 994	25 053	17 480	7 855	921
Ireland[j]	5 164	15 674		21 226	108	2 691
Italy[j]	108 231	276 553	291 694	51 611	203 843	41 271
Japan	108 767	457 767	304 167	328 265	..	14 462
Netherlands	1 459	84 999[c]	..	52 162	54 457	..
New Zealand[h,f]	7 898	16 547	..	19 050	..	..
Norway	5 640	50 299[d]	..	23 972	..	3 828
Portugal[f]	5 640	70 897	..	43 274	..	..
Spain	39 217	116 098	80 130	74 918	53 950	5 164
Sweden	74 700	94 100[d]		58 172	27 400[k]	4 500
Turkey	6 293	216 859	42 423	46 204		708
United Kingdom[h,j]	26 000	213 000	129 000	176 000	100 000[l]	20 345
United States[h,f]	..	1 425 000		1 042 000[d]	..	..
Yugoslavia	39 293	62 254	76 678	57 391	..	4 676[m]

a) Includes some teachers in teacher training; for Norway and Yugoslavia, technical/vocational teachers at this level are included with those in general streams, while only those technical/vocational teachers who are in specific institutions for these subjects are counted separately. For the Netherlands, this column includes teachers at the third level, while for the United Kingdom, teachers in public non-advanced further education are also included here.
b) Full-time equivalents.
c) Includes pre-primary.
d) Includes second level/first stage.
e) Includes pre-primary teachers and teachers in schools providing both first level and second level/first stage education.
f) 1985/86.
g) Public sector only.
h) Includes teachers in private pre-primary.
i) 1984/85.
j) Data supplied by national authorities.
k) Includes general education at this level.
l) Estimated number of lecturers in non-advanced further education.
m) Primary education only.

Source: OECD (1989), Education in OECD Countries 1986-87: A Compendium of Statistical Information, Paris, Tables 2.1-2.6.

TEACHER NUMBERS: A SHRINKING PROFESSION?

Factors influencing trends in teacher numbers

Moving beyond the snapshot picture in Table 1 to consider *trends*, the direction of change in numbers of teachers employed is dependent at any one time on a variety of factors, that may be mutually reinforcing or in conflict with one another. Among these, the most obvious are: the evolution of numbers of youngsters of school and college age who are pupils and students, enrolment rates in the various branches of education and training outside the compulsory school years and any changes in the legal definitions of when these years begin or terminate, staffing ratios, spending priorities, and rates of staff recruitment, wastage, and retirement. Trends are determined, that is, by a variety of factors beyond the demographic shifts which have exercised such publicised influence on the demand for teachers and which accounted for the desperate search for new staff in the 1960s and 1970s (the timing varied by country) and the sharp reduction of subsequent recruitment levels in many countries. Recognising the multiplicity of influences, it is nevertheless instructive to consider, as background to changing teacher numbers, the demographic changes which have occurred over the past couple of decades, and this we do using two indicators: trends in recorded numbers of births, and the evolution of numbers of young people in school-age bands since the 1960s (Tables 2 and 3).

Demographic developments

Several interesting features stand out from these tables. First, in all countries except Australia and Sweden, the number of births has fallen in the quarter century following the beginning of the 1960s and even in those exceptional cases, the 1987 level of births was down from previous peaks. Second, this drop varied very widely as can be seen by comparing those countries where it has been of the order of 30 per cent or more (Austria, Germany, Greece, Italy, Portugal and Spain) with those where only very modest change was discernible between these two years (Ireland, France), though simply comparing end points masks quite wide variations in births over this period as the experience of the latter two countries well illustrates. Third, while most countries have witnessed a drop in the number of 5-9 year-olds since the beginning of the 1980s, which is already becoming felt as falling secondary school rolls, there are, on the other hand, clear divergences in the trend in births over the same period. Of the 23 countries covered by Table 2, births rose in 10 countries and fell in 12, though in general the tendency to increase, where it was in evidence, was much weaker than the opposite one of falling births. The decline in births has been particularly noticeable this decade in Ireland (a 20 per cent drop between 1980 and 1987) and in the Mediterranean countries of Greece (28 per cent), Italy (15 per cent), Spain (23 per cent), and in Portugal (24 per cent). These examples serve as a reminder that identical demographic pressures are not operating in all countries, particularly in terms of the timing of the rise and fall of numbers of given school-age populations. It should also be added that in some countries, migratory movements are sufficiently important to exercise a significant effect on student numbers, over and above the main demographic variable of births.

Having thus examined some basic demographic facts and whatever their impact on the *future* demand for teachers, has there been evidence up to now of a corresponding decline in

18

Table 2
EVOLUTION OF BIRTHS IN SELECTED YEARS
1960-1987 (in 000s)

Country	1960	1965	1970	1975	1980	1987	% change 1960-1987
Australia	230	223	258	233	226	244	+ 6
Austria	126	130	112	94	91	87	− 31
Belgium	156	155	141	119	125	117	− 25
Canada	479	419	370	358	371	372	− 22
Denmark	76	86	71	72	57	56	− 26
Finland	82	78	65	66	63	60	− 27
France	816	862	850	745	800	768	− 5
Germany	969	1 044	811	601	621	642	− 34
Greece	157	151	145	142	148	106	− 32
Iceland	49	47	40	44	45	42	− 14
Ireland	61	63	64	68	74	59	− 3
Italy	923	1 108	917	842	658	560	− 39
Japan	1 606	1 839	1 948	1 897	1 589	1 354	− 16
Luxembourg	50	53	44	40	42	42	− 16
Netherlands	239	245	239	178	181	187	− 22
New Zealand	63	60	62	57	51	55	− 13
Norway	62	66	65	56	51	54	− 13
Portugal	214	210	181	180	161	123	− 43
Spain	655	668	656	669	566	435[a]	− 34
Sweden	102	123	110	104	97	105	+ 3
Switzerland	94	112	99	79	74	77	− 18
United Kingdom	918	997	904	698	754	775	− 15
United States	4 307	3 801	3 739	3 144	3 589	3 829	− 11

a) 1986.
Source: OECD Demographic Statistics.

teacher numbers? Did the demographic shifts that marked substantial falls in pupil and student numbers in many countries result, in the words of the title of this section, in a "shrinking profession"? There is, in fact, very little evidence that they did.

Little sign yet of declining numbers of teachers in many countries

Some countries have actually experienced dramatic growth of their teacher numbers. In *Greece*, they approximately doubled between 1970 and 1986 (from an index of 100 to 195 by the school year 1986/87)[4]. This was especially marked in general secondary schools where teacher numbers rose from under 13 000 to 41 321 over this period. Even in the other school sectors, the growth was still significant if somewhat less spectacular: pre-primary, 2 748 to 7 371; primary, 29 336 to 36 301; technical and vocational, 4 915 to 7 547. Australian, Austrian, Danish, French, and United States statistics tell a similar story, even if the rates of increase have been somewhat more modest. Teacher numbers have continued to grow in *Australia*, if at slower rates than in the 1960s and early 1970s, and this has been

Table 3
NUMBERS OF YOUNG PEOPLE [IN HUNDRED THOUSANDS]
AGED 5-9, 10-14, AND 15-19 YEARS IN OECD COUNTRIES
1960, 1970, 1980, 1987

Country	Aged 5-9				Aged 10-14				Aged 15-19			
	1960	1970	1980	1987	1960	1970	1980	1987	1960	1970	1980	1987
Australia	10.2	12.3	13.1	11.9	9.8	11.9	12.7	12.7	7.7	11.0	13.1	13.9
Austria	4.8	6.4	5.0	4.4	5.0	5.7	6.1	4.6	5.9	4.8	6.5	5.8
Belgium	7.1	7.9	6.4	6.0	6.9	7.7	7.2	6.2	5.4	7.3	7.9	7.0
Canada	20.3	22.9	18.0	18.1	17.8	22.9	19.5	17.9	13.7	20.6	23.6	19.1
Denmark	3.7	3.9	3.6	2.9	4.2	3.7	3.9	3.5	3.8	3.7	4.0	3.7
Finland	4.4	3.8	3.0	3.2	4.9	4.0	3.5	3.1	3.7	4.3	3.8	3.3
France	40.1	42.6	41.1	38.3	40.3	41.7	41.7	39.3	27.8	41.6	42.9	42.9
Germany	38.3	49.9	33.9	28.9	34.8	43.5	48.7	29.3	39.0	40.0	52.2	43.4
Greece	7.1	7.0	7.0	7.2^a	7.2	7.1	7.8	7.0^a	6.3	6.6	7.2	7.7^a
Iceland	0.2	..	0.2	0.2^a	0.2	..	0.2	0.2^a	0.1	..	0.2	0.2^a
Ireland	2.9	3.1	3.5	3.5	2.9	2.9	3.9	3.5	2.3	2.8	3.2	3.3
Italy	40.3	45.5	43.2	36.1^b	43.0	40.8	45.7	43.9^b	38.1	38.6	45.8	47.1^b
Japan	..	..	99.8	80.2	..	..	89.1	97.0	..	..	81.9	96.3
Luxembourg	..	..	0.2	0.2^a	..	..	0.3	0.2^a	..	..	0.3	0.3^a
Netherlands	11.0	12.1	10.5	8.9	11.7	11.6	12.2	9.5	9.1	11.1	12.5	12.1
New Zealand	2.6	3.1	2.9	2.5	2.4	3.0	3.0	2.8	1.8	2.6	3.1	3.0
Norway	3.0	3.1	3.1	2.6	3.2	3.1	3.3	2.9	2.6	3.1	3.1	3.3
Portugal	8.5	..	8.3	7.6	8.3	..	8.6	8.7	7.5	..	8.4	8.6
Spain	26.9	31.7	32.8	28.7	26.2	30.2	32.3	32.8	24.1	26.9	31.8	32.9
Sweden	5.4	5.6	5.6	4.8	6.2	5.3	5.8	5.3	5.7	5.5	5.7	5.7
Switzerland	4.0	4.9	4.0	3.7	4.2	4.6	4.8	3.8	4.1	4.7	5.1	4.7
Turkey	38.5	49.0	59.0	62.0	31.0	44.2	54.6	60.4	23.2	37.2	48.8	55.7
United Kingdom	38.0	46.8	38.9	35.5	42.6	41.1	45.3	35.1	35.7	38.5	47.0	43.8
United States	188.1	199.2	166.1	176.6	169.2	208.5	182.4	164.8	134.4	193.3	211.6	185.0

a) 1986.
b) 1985.
Source: OECD Demographic Statistics.

particularly marked in the non-government (private) sector employing over 50 000 full-time equivalent teachers in 1988, compared with 37 200 in 1987, and a little under 30 000 in 1976[5]. In *Austria*, the moderate increases in the stock of primary school teachers (1965: 23 635; 1970: 24 815; 1980: 27 525; 1987: 28 652) are far out-stripped by the growth of teaching personnel in secondary education[6]. Taking only the years 1965 and 1987, the increases were of the following magnitudes: compulsory secondary, 11 562 to 33 233; academic upper secondary, 6 096 to 17 285; vocational middle and higher schools, 9 651 to 21 713. Teaching has here clearly remained a growth occupation. The *Danish* statistics[7] show a steady increase in numbers of teachers in primary and lower secondary schools (*Folkeskole*) from just under 54 000 in the mid-1970s to a little under 65 000 by school year 1980/81 and up again to 67 279 by 1985/86. And the *French* figures reinforce the same pattern. Taking teachers in the public sector, in primary schools and secondary schools (*collèges* and *lycées*) respectively, the figures stood at 235 198 and 102 894 in 1962/63, 272 482 and 223 228 in 1972/73, 299 823 and 296 424 in 1983/84, rising finally to 303 483 and 303 827 teachers in public primary and secondary schools by the academic

20

year 1986/87[8]. There is little sign here of a shrinking profession, still less considering the declared official aim in France to double the proportion of youngsters who complete secondary education to the level of the *baccalauréat* or its equivalent from the present level of a little over 40 to 80 per cent by the year 2000.

In the most populous of OECD countries and the one where teachers have been under the policy spotlight perhaps more pointedly than any other – the *United States* – a background fact to the fears increasingly expressed there about future shortages is that their schools have never employed as many teachers as they do now. In the entire school system, K (kindergarten) through to year 12 in high school, the 1986 figure of 2 591 000 and that projected for 1987 of 2 630 000 stand against 2 485 000 in 1980, 2 451 000 in 1975, and less than two million prior to 1966[9]. The increases have been most marked at the elementary level, while dropping slightly from peak years for total secondary school teachers employed in the mid- and late 1970s.

Even in those countries where trends in teacher numbers have been less expansionary, evidence still shows mixed developments rather than declining numbers across the board. This can be seen in the cases of four other major OECD countries: Canada, Germany, Japan, and the United Kingdom. The *Canadian* total for primary and secondary teachers in 1983/84 was slightly down on the peak year of 1977/78 (192 128 compared with 196 037) but still higher than 1974 levels and before[10], while the decline of numbers of full-time teachers in publicly-maintained schools in the *United Kingdom* from 499 000 in 1975/76 to 464 000 in 1986/87 has been most clearly felt in the primary sector (240 to 203 000 as opposed to secondary teacher numbers (259 000 rising to 260 000), though totals for teachers employed have more recently been falling in secondary schools too since the beginning of the 1980s[11]. For *Japan*, given the demographic developments charted in Tables 2 and 3 (births declined from 1 948 000 in 1970 to 1 354 000 in 1987), it is not surprising that there are fewer teachers at the pre-primary and primary levels now than before. But the fall is still barely perceptible in kindergartens – 98 000 teachers in 1987 compared with about 101 000 at the turn of the decade – though the trend is clearly downward in primary schools (449 000 in 1987 compared with 474 000 in 1983). In lower and upper secondary schools, however, the graphs have yet to peak and the 1987 levels of 292 057 and 274 913 full-time teachers represent record numbers[12].

Even *Germany*, an OECD country which experienced one of the most dramatic falls in births and birthrates in the 1960s and 1970s, the expected decline in teachers employed in primary and lower secondary schools can still be set against a recent upturn in primary school teaching staff (110 400 in 1983 rising to 115 100 in 1987), the long-term overall increase in upper secondary grammar schools (the 1987 level of 54 000 being two-thirds higher than that of a decade before at less than 34 000) and the trend in vocational schools – 64 000 full-time equivalent teachers in 1975 compared with nearly 90 000 in vocational establishments by 1987 – is growth of comparable order[13].

The extent to which teacher numbers have held up, even against substantial shifts in pupil and student enrolments, should not be exaggerated, however, and the timing of the progress of the demographic bulge, with falling numbers of youngsters in its wake, through education systems and beyond has varied. In some cases, therefore, countries that have yet to experience falling teacher numbers may still do so in the face of the sheer scale of the declining rolls. Yet a general thesis of a shrinking occupation – of decline in numbers as well as the much reported slump in professional satisfaction and professional status levels – receives little support from the evidence.

The two factors (teacher status and numbers) may not, of course, be unrelated. Small numbers help to establish high status. But while this may hold in comparing the fortunes of a "mass" occupation and a small professional body, it is probably less significant in accounting for changes *within* teaching itself over the years. It has never been, in modern times, a small professional group in OECD countries.

FALLING PUPIL/TEACHER RATIOS (PTRs)

The general trends

Given the developments outlined above – in particular, a substantial fall in number of school-age youngsters and the relatively buoyant teacher numbers in most OECD countries – it was only natural that pupil/teacher ratios have correspondingly fallen where those were the observed trends. The evidence does indeed show that this fall of PTRs has been the predominant experience, though there are reported exceptions taking all OECD countries into account.

In some countries, this fall has been persistent and long-standing. The *United States* figures show just such a trend, the bigger drop being seen in elementary schooling where, in public and private schools, the PTR fell from 31.4 in 1955 to 28.4 by 1965, continuing to drop to 21.7 in 1975, and down still further to 18.8 by 1986. The corresponding figures for secondary schools for these years were 20.3, 20.6, 18.6, and 15.8[14]. The German, Greek, and Danish data follow the pattern. In *Germany*, the fall has been especially marked in primary schools and the non-selective secondary schools (36.7 in 1960, 33.1 in 1965, 27.3 a decade later, falling to 17.8 midway through the 1980s) though the same trend is apparent for all other types of school. The drop has been least apparent in vocational schools in recent years where earlier very marked gains in the late 1960s and early 1970s (from as high as 47.4 in 1965, dropping to 39.6 in 1970 and still further to 33.8 by the mid-1970s) have slowed and the 1985 figure was only a little down on the mid-1970s level at 29.3[15]. Given the very marked increases in teacher numbers in *Greece* described above, it could only be expected that pupil/teacher ratios dropped sharply, as indeed they did. In public schools, comparisons for the school years 1970/71 and 1986/87 show respectively: 31.9 to 19.6 in pre-primary education, 31.5 to 23.5 at the primary level, 33.8 to 17.9 in general secondary schools, and 18.6 to 14.7 in technical and vocational schools. (The equivalent figures in the private sphere, for the same two reference years, were: 30.5 and 25.2, 26.7 and 24.4, 31.9 and 13.7, 27.9 and 12.3)[16]. The marked differences in PTRs seen in many countries by school level and between the public and private sectors are illustrated in this particular case, though in recent years the sharper variations have tended to flatten out. *Danish* data confirm the overall story: over the decade since 1975/76, the corresponding ratio dropped from a little under 15 (14.9) in primary and folk high schools to 10.6[17].

Other country examples serve to underline the general trend. The *Netherlands* national report describes a drop in the PTR for primary schools from 23.6 in 1977 to 19.6 in the mid-1980s but in this case alongside a relatively stable ratio in secondary schools[18]. A similar improvement, though now slowing, of change in PTRs can also be seen in *Australia* though stable government secondary school figures contrast with continued falling teacher/pupil ratios in the private sector[19]. *United Kingdom* trends for public sector schools (the predominant majority of schools in the system) are gradual and consistent, with the biggest drop in the PTRs occurring in the pre-primary and primary levels. Taking the years

1965/66, 1975/76, and 1986/87, the ratios stood at 27.8, 22.1, and 21.2 for pre-primary education, 28.2, 23.8, 21.8 in primary schooling, and 18.0, 16.8, and 15.4 at the secondary level[20]. And *Swedish* data, in this case presented conversely as teacher/pupil ratios, show that since the mid-1970s, this has risen from around 7.6 in 1977/78 to a little over 8.7 by 1985/86[21].

Variations and caveats

Having thus sketched the general trends, a number of comments and caveats must be made. First, it is clear that there are differences in staffing ratios by level and type of schooling and by whether the provision is public or private. Recent *Australian* figures bear this out: for example, in 1988, the government public schools enjoyed lower PTRs across both primary and secondary schooling over non-government schools (18.0 compared with 20.3 at the primary level; 12.2 compared with 13.6 for secondary schools)[19]. A further commonality across OECD education systems is that the PTRs in secondary schools are lower than at the primary level while, in all, special schools require significantly more staff per student. For example, the equivalent PTRs in special schools in *Australia* for 1986 were 4.8 and 4.4[22], while in *Germany*, it was less than 7 in 1986/87, having stood at over 20 only a quarter of a century before, and the figure for the *United Kingdom* in 1984/85 was approximately the same (6.8) having fallen from 11.1 in the mid-1960s and 8.7 in the mid-1970s. And, of course, there are important regional and school-by-school differences in staffing ratios brought about by a wide range of factors.

The purpose of drawing attention to these differences between levels and sectors is partly a technical one, underlining that the global averages mask a wealth of important variation. But there is a more substantial point to be made: changes in observed figures follow too from new policy directions. That may be a deliberate policy decision about class size or teacher numbers. For instance, 1987 legislation in Italy established upper (25 pupils) and lower (15 pupils) limits to the beginning class size of each level of schooling[23]. It may be the deliberate expansion of "teacher-intensive" levels of the education system (or their contraction). And it may follow from policies aimed at specific target groups. For example, to the degree that the integration of handicapped pupils into ordinary schools is a matter of general policy[24], then a drop of PTRs in those schools would only be expected, as the already-low ratios in special schooling demonstrate that this type of teaching is especially demanding of resources and human effort. These different components are illustrated by developments cited in the Italian and Norwegian national reports:

"Significant change has occurred in the past four years: alongside an overall drop of 300,000 pupils has been an increase of 14,000 teachers. This has arisen for a number of reasons: the phenomenon of repeating school years and of some falling behind increases the size of the relevant school cohort at the compulsory level; there has been a growth of upper secondary school students; the generalisation of full-time schooling throughout the system; the integration of handicapped pupils; the maintenance of low pupil-teacher ratios (14 to 1 in primary schools and 10 to 1 in secondary schools in 1982)"[25].

and

"This gives a pupil/teacher ratio of 9.9. The reasons for this development are partly decisions about fewer pupils per class, decreases in the number of lessons teachers are supposed to teach, need for more teachers due to integration of handicapped children etc., i.e. intended increases in educational expenses. However, an important reason is the fact that in a highly decentralised school system, reduction in pupil numbers will have very limited effect on the number of teachers: even though the number of 7-graders in a school drops from 20 to 14, they cannot be bussed 40 kilometres to the neighbouring school, and cannot be taught with the 8-graders"[26].

The point to be underlined is twofold. First, a fall in PTRs can only be interpreted as a sign of improved conditions of teaching when analysis of the context supports such an interpretation; in some circumstances, the growing demands on teachers may mean that such a fall is only sufficient for conditions to remain approximately equivalent to where they previously stood. Second, there is the related point that any simple comparisons of aggregate numbers of pupils and teachers can be usefully broken down into the component parts that explain it.

It is no doubt a reasonable assessment that the size of the observed falls in pupil/teacher ratios do represent an improvement over the clearly under-staffed systems of the immediate post-war years and of the 1950s and 1960s. But the evidence suggests too that there are marked differences between countries and within systems in their staffing levels. And reported exceptions to the general improvements in PTRs, combined with concern about the emergence of teacher shortages in the future as discussed in the next chapter, serve as a reminder that there is no guarantee that observed trends will not be reversed in the face of new conditions. But more than this we cannot say with precision in this chapter. The figures presented in this section, let it be reiterated once more, are calculated on very differing bases, using various definitions and populations. For this reason, they do *not* permit close comparisons between countries. Careful cross-national comparative study is needed if the magnitudes of country differences are to be properly revealed.

Careful analysis of the benefits and potential of smaller PRTs would also be valuable. The benefits of smaller classes – such as greater contact between the student and teacher and the freeing of capacity for the vital tasks of class preparation and INSET – need to be underlined. It is probably fair to assert that, despite those benefits, education systems that have experienced dropping PTRs have not fully and actively exploited the advantages thereby opened up. But it is probably also fair to assert that those benefits must be evaluated in relation to other uses of educational resources. As class sizes diminish, the trade-offs with alternative uses of scarce funds need to be appraised. It is not to be assumed that continually falling pupil/teacher ratios must always be sought once reasonable class sizes are assured when there are so many other claims on educational resources.

THE AGE FACTOR: THE "GREYING" OF THE TEACHING FORCE

Alongside the label "a feminised profession" (see next section), a common description of teachers today is that, taken overall, they are ageing. The teaching occupation is now typically portrayed as "greying". Perhaps because today's world sets so much store by youthfulness, such a description carries an implicit note of alarm. But is the teaching force ageing? And should this trend, if it is occurring, be a source of concern? The evidence allows some response to the former question. Answers to the latter – should this, where it is occurring, be a source of alarm? – is more difficult to resolve and is, in any event, more a qualitative than a quantitative matter. The evidence nevertheless does provide some indication of issues and questions that touch on matters at the heart of the subsequent chapters such as teacher supply, the issue of maintaining quality, and the capacity of existing staff to meet new challenges.

The complex components of the statistic "average age of teachers"

A number of quite different components combine in determining the overall average age of the teaching force. Fewer very young entrants (aged, for example, 19, 20 or 21) coming into teaching may be the result simply of the higher qualification levels demanded from initial studies and training, which necessarily makes starting teachers older. This factor alone will raise the average. Since this trend has been a deliberate aim of policy in many countries, often supported by teachers and their representatives themselves, it would be contradictory to view this source of ageing with alarm nor is it any indicator of lack of "new blood". On the other hand, fewer young entrants and a rising average age may instead reflect insufficient openings for young teachers (cool demand) or the reluctance of young graduates to take up teaching as a career (insufficient supply). These are certainly more legitimate causes of disquiet.

An overall rising average age can be the reflection of factors affecting teachers in mid-career such as a lower wastage rate of those leaving the profession entirely as opportunities become scarce elsewhere in the labour market, or through a reduction in the number of promotional openings within education but outside the classroom itself, such as in educational administration. (Whether these different sources of ageing are to be judged positively or negatively – in terms of the relative numbers of high or poor quality teachers staying or leaving the school system, or of the merits of movement of personnel as a good in itself – cannot be decided upon in the abstract but only on the basis of concrete evidence). The average age is likely to rise too if more women remain in teaching without taking a substantial break from work for family reasons as is increasingly the pattern. And it rises if more entrants are recruited from alternative routes from the traditional path through initial training insofar as such entrants tend to be older adults recruited from other occupations and backgrounds. Once again, evidence of ageing by itself cannot be assumed to be negative; several of these developments are being positively encouraged in a range of countries.

Concerning the older end of the age spectrum, the aggregate average will rise if larger numbers of older teachers move through towards the twilight of their careers without being counterbalanced by a comparable body of younger recruits or if fewer take early retirement than before. The extent and availability of early retirement remains both a policy lever and a largely unknown factor in predicting future teacher numbers. Growing proportions of teachers aged over, for example, 45 years are an indicator of significantly greater policy relevance if the majority of the teaching force will be retiring in their mid to late fifties than if they are due to remain on well into their sixties. In fact, the very concepts of careers in and retirement from teaching merit close attention; it shall be argued in the next chapter that it is now timely to consider ways of breaking away from the predominant practice of teachers having to be in either full-time work or full-time retirement.

Signs of ageing among teachers

For all these reasons, the indicator "average age of teachers" is at best a blunt instrument of understanding, and this needs to be borne in mind in interpreting the

25

evidence. There are distinct signs that the average is rising in some countries. In the North American countries of Canada and the United States, this trend is very clear. In *Canada*, in a little over the decade between 1972/73 to 1983/84, the average age of elementary and high school teachers had gone up substantially from 35 to 39 years old[27]. Reflecting the different components that influence the mean age, as discussed above, the Canadian statistical report notes that this rise is at least partly accounted for by a drop in the proportion of teachers under 25 years old from 17 per cent at the beginning of this period to only 2 per cent by 1983/84. *Digest of Education Statistics* figures published for the *United States* depict a very similar trend and allow a longer time perspective in this case deploying the median rather than the mean age, a median of only 33 years in 1976 had risen to 41 by 1986[28].

The longer time data in the *United States* case is distinctly revealing, though, since it shows that the 1961 median age for U.S. teachers was exactly the same at 41 years old. This comparison points to an important qualification to the concern expressed about the "greying" of the profession: observing trends from the mid-1970s (depending on the country in question) automatically skews the analysis through beginning with a misleadingly low starting point given the massive recruitment of young teachers that was undertaken in the 1960s and early 1970s in many countries. On this argument, the observed ageing of teachers is in part simply a return to an historical norm. But noting the distortion introduced by using the mid-1970s as the comparison date cannot, however, be taken as grounds on its own to allay the concern being expressed in some quarters that insufficient numbers of young teachers are entering to avert a possible crisis of supply in the future. It is only to note that information on the rising average age of teachers over a relatively short time span gives an exaggerated picture of ageing.

The same United States statistics provide another interesting qualification to the general picture presented by the averages and also a contrast with another Member country for which relevant data are available – *Austria*. The Austrian report shows a marked difference in the age structure of men and women teachers[29]. There, women teachers are clearly younger than their male colleagues, reflecting the tendency for women to leave for family reasons, sometimes never to return. The United States figures show that in the past women in the classroom were significantly *older* on average than the men and the 1961 female median age of 46 years old stands in stark contrast with the male median of 34 years for that year! This earlier gender gap has since disappeared and there were doubtless a variety of explanatory factors behind that marked divergence that probably included a tendency for women teachers at that time not to marry and the ample opportunities for men to be promoted out of the classroom into administration. Whatever the explanation, the example suggests that such key variables as age, gender, the attractiveness of teaching, the availability of alternative employment, and the supply of new recruits to teaching, come together in complex combinations that can differ significantly from country to country, and also from one era to another.

Evidence of "ageing" but not "aged"

Is the ageing process observed in the North American countries reproduced elsewhere? Evidence from Australia, Japan, the United Kingdom, and France provide at least partial qualification to alarmist notions of an occupation on the verge of decrepitude. For *Australia* (Victoria), marked redistributions between younger and middle-aged teachers in primary and secondary schools over recent years – approximately 55 per cent under 30 years of age in both sectors in 1976 had fallen to 19.2 and 23.7 per cent respectively by 1987 – saw only moderate increases in teacher average age. In primary schools, it rose from 32.1 to 36.6 years, while at the secondary level the increase was from 32.8 to 35.8 years[30]. The percentage of full-time teachers aged 45 years and older has actually *fallen* for *Japanese* primary school teachers since the mid-1970s (42.2 down to 36.1 per cent by 1983), while remaining relatively stable among lower secondary school teachers over this short period (36.7 to 37.3) though the proportion did rise slightly at the upper secondary level (34.2 to 36.5 per cent)[31]. Since the beginning of the decade, those 45 and over have risen from 30 to 34 per cent for women full-time teachers in the *United Kingdom*, but have remained at 30 per cent for full-time male teachers in primary and secondary schools between 1979/80 and 1985/86[32]. And in *France*, the proportion of secondary teachers in public schools aged 45 and over stood at less than a quarter in 1984/85[33]. Among French primary school teachers in the public sector, the median age for women was 36 years and for men 37 years in 1986/87 (the equivalent statistic for both sexes in secondary schools was 38 in the same year)[34]. On the basis of this evidence, it would certainly be an exaggeration to describe the teaching force as "aged" as well as ageing. These latter statistics referring to proportions of older teachers provide also more pertinent indicators of "greying" than overall means or medians which compound, as we have seen, quite diverse developments.

Yet some of the same national examples can be deployed to illustrate vividly how the picture can change when a slightly different indicator is used. In the United Kingdom, for instance, comparing proportions of teachers over 40 instead of 45 years old, shows a much more distinct and rapid ageing pattern (women teachers: 43 per cent aged 40 and over in 1979/80 had risen to 48 per cent by 1985/86; for men: 41 per cent in 1979/80 had gone up to 44 per cent). Indeed, the CERI report for England and Wales describes these changes and their rapidity starkly: "From the period 1985 to 1990, the age structure of the teaching force is projected to alter with an increase of the proportion aged over 40 from 46 per cent to 57 per cent"[35]. This, surely, is rapid change. Detailed analyses of *French* teachers reiterate the point that it is not so much the current age structure that is worrying but how that structure may likely transform over the next decade that is a cause for concern[36]. The conclusions to be drawn here are twofold: first, capsule descriptions of teachers as an already "aged" professional group are often exaggerated; second, with the passage of time those labels may well become, without significant counter-measures, increasingly apt.

In certain other Member countries, the aged adjective is still an inappropriate one to apply to teachers. The *Dutch* report describes a slight increase in the mean age for primary school teachers but they remain relatively young (34.8 years old on average having risen from 32.9 in 1978). The mean age stands at 39.6 years at the secondary level having gone up by approximately one year since 1978[37]. The *Danish* national report indicates that approximately half of the primary and lower secondary school teachers are under the age of 35[38] while the *German* report describes a situation in Hesse where 6 out of 10 teachers are under 40 years, a situation observed to be typical of other *Länder*[39]. The situation among *Irish* primary teachers in 1987 was not dissimilar – 45.6 per cent below 35 years rising to 59.7 under 40's. Among secondary school teachers, however, the respective percentages were 35.4 and 45.2 and the average age nearly 40 years[40]. And in Greece, with its notable expansion of teacher numbers described above, the proportion of teachers under 40 years in general secondary education has remained at over 7 out of 10 since the early 1970s, though it has fallen somewhat in primary schooling (59 in 1973/74 to 54.7 per cent by 1984/85)[41].

Returning then to the general questions that introduced this section – "is teaching a greying profession and, if it is, should this cause alarm?" – the evidence suggests a mixed response. On the whole, teaching forces in OECD countries are ageing but from an artificially low starting point if the mid-1970s is the comparison. It is still a relatively young professional body in some countries. The worries expressed in some quarters about lack of "new blood" and possible sudden future teacher shortages address issues that are, as yet, medium- to long-term, admitting still of sustained long-term solutions where analysis suggests that problems are likely to arise. But if this should be mistaken as grounds for complacency, it needs to be added that as long-term phenomena they are correspondingly less amenable to immediate solutions when the time comes. Lack of "fresh blood", by its very nature, cannot be rectified overnight. The budgetary implications of ageing should also be signalled. With incremental salary scales, a higher average age for teachers leads, other things being equal, to greater expenditure.

We return to these issues in the subsequent chapters. To conclude this section, it can be emphasized that the "ageing" question raises a number of distinct issues that do not necessarily carry either the same implications or solutions. It is necessary to distinguish clearly between the relatively intangible if real factor of insufficient recruitment of new teachers to bring vitality and "fresh blood" into classrooms from the planning question of attracting adequate numbers of new staff to fill vacant posts each year. And in neither case should it be assumed that younger teachers are better than older ones, a consideration rarely mentioned in discussions of ageing and renewal. Those analyses characterising teaching as a craft learned over many years' experience[42] would suggest that, if anything, the opposite is true. And this issue relates in turn to the important one of deciding how teachers are to be appraised: what emphasis should be placed on pedagogical skills and subject knowledge? Should all the teachers be assessed against the same criteria or should the experienced be considered differently from the relative novices? But lack of "fresh blood" and a gradually ageing teaching force nevertheless raise sharply the question of how the profession is to keep abreast of change. The importance of in-service education and training here is obvious.

THE POSITION OF WOMEN IN TEACHING

Whether or not the epithet "feminised" can accurately be used to describe the profession (discussed below), teaching is an occupation that employs very many women in all OECD countries. It is also one where the prospects and career paths of women and men typically so diverge that the special conditions and problems confronting women cannot be assumed to be representative of those applying to teachers as a whole. Indeed, this fact alone raises the matter of the appropriateness of addressing teachers as a single profession. The point to be underlined here is that since women make up such a sizeable proportion of the teaching staffs of OECD countries, as well as of the pool of potential entrants not presently teaching, any policies addressing such key matters as improving attractiveness, increasing supply, or enhancing quality, must have women as a specific and prominent target. The special position of women in teaching thus deserves detailed consideration, and the rest of this chapter is devoted to this exercise.

A diverse picture

The overall (if incomplete) picture portrayed by Table 4, showing the proportion of women teachers, aggregating full- or part-time posts in the different levels of OECD

Table 4
THE PERCENTAGE OF WOMEN TEACHERS IN OECD COUNTRIES BY LEVEL[a] OF EDUCATION
1986/87

Country	Pre-primary	First level	Second level first stage	Second level second stage general	Special
Australia[b]	..	70.9	..	47.3	75.2
Austria	99.6	79.9	59.3	52.2	..
Belgium	..	75.6[c]	..	51.3[d]	..
Canada	..	68.9[e]	..	45.5[f]	..
Denmark[g]	96.0	59.0	59.0	37.0	..
France	96.1[h]	71.3[i]	60.8[h]	49.5[h]	..
Germany	91.4	79.2	48.1	30.6	63.2
Greece[j]	100.0	48.9	62.4	46.6	61.3
Ireland[j]	75.9	76.0	..	..	75.6
Italy[k]	95.0	88.9	67.6	62.5	..
Japan	88.2	56.3	34.8	22.1	49.3
Netherlands	..	63.5[g]	..	27.5	49.4
New Zealand[b j]	..	70.6	..	46.8	..
Norway	..	59.8	..	34.1	65.8
Spain	96.0	72.6	51.4	50.2	72.8
Sweden[g]	95.6[l]	82.3	48.0	52.0	80.0[m]
Turkey	99.5	41.8	32.4	41.9	36.6
United Kingdom	100.0	78.4	50.4	50.6	69.0
Yugoslavia	94.4[j]	71.3	53.7	47.4	71.5

a) The data on teachers in technical-vocational education from Table 2.5 of the report on which this table is based cover such a broad range of programmes including secondary, post-secondary, and teacher training, and this varying from country to country, that they have been excluded from this table.
b) Of full-time equivalents.
c) Includes pre-primary.
d) Includes second level-first stage.
e) Includes teachers in schools providing solely pre-primary education and the first six grades (not first level teachers in schools catering for both first and second levels).
f) Includes teachers in schools catering solely for grades 7 to 13.
g) Data supplied by national authorities for 1988.
h) Public sector only.
i) Includes private pre-primary.
j) 1985/86.
k) 1984/85.
l) Includes personnel in leisure centres for 7-12 year-olds.
m) Compulsory schools only.
Sources: OECD (1989), *Education in OECD Countries 1986-87: A Compendium of Statistical Information,* Paris, Tables 2.1 to 2.4, 2.6 and data supplied by national authorities.

education systems up to the end of the secondary phase, shows that the common description of a "feminised profession" belies a more complex reality. The share of teaching posts held by women varies markedly from the pre-primary and primary levels to the different sectors of secondary education, as it does across countries. Trends vary too: in some countries, the share of teaching posts held by men and women has been relatively stable or the female balance has actually fallen, while in others the tendency to feminisation has grown stronger. And whatever the aggregate figures show, full account must be taken of the striking differences between the sexes in their success in gaining access to promotions and leadership positions.

Whether or not "feminisation" is an accurate term and whether it is judged to be high or low depends on which criterion is employed. Arguably, feminisation should be assumed present only when women make up a substantial majority of an occupation. A less demanding criterion would be that it is present when they comprise more than half the workers in it. A different approach is instead to compare the proportion of women in an occupation against the overall female share of employment in that country (a case of a low female presence in teaching posts in one country compared with others may indicate more about women's employment in general in that country than about their situation in teaching *per*

Table 5
FEMALE LABOUR FORCE PARTICIPATION RATES: 1967-1987,
AND THE FEMALE SHARE OF TOTAL EMPLOYMENT IN 1987

Country	Female labour force participation rates (%)			Total numbers in employment (000s)	Female percentage of total employment
	1967	1977	1987	1987	1987
Australia	44	52	57	7 745	39.7
Austria	50[a]	48	53	3 430	40.1
Belgium	39	45	51[d]	4 217	40.7
Canada	41	52	65	13 200	43.2
Denmark	55	65	76[d]	2 799	45.9
Finland	60	68	73	2 583	47.1
France	47	53	56	24 073	42.5
Germany	48	49	52	28 216	39.3
Greece	31[b]	33	41[e]	3 884	35.9
Ireland	35	34	37[d]	1 319	30.9
Italy	33	38	43	24 031	36.1
Japan	57	53	58	60 840	39.9
Luxembourg	34[c]	39	44[d]	167[d]	34.1
Netherlands	..	32	41[d]	5 933	35.2
New Zealand	37	43	47[e]	1 620	42.2
Norway	37	58	72	2 171	44.3
Portugal	25	55	58	4 522	41.6
Spain	30[c]	33	37	14 675	32.6
Sweden	55	70	80	4 421	48.0
Switzerland	51	52	54[d]	3 297	37.3
United Kingdom	50	56	62	28 212	41.4
United States	46	55	66	122 122	44.1
OECD total				382 915[f]	41.2

a) 1968.
b) 1970.
c) 1971.
d) 1986.
e) 1985.
f) Includes Iceland and Turkey.
Note: The female labour force participation rate is defined in this table as the female labour force of all ages divided by the female population aged 15-64.
Sources: OECD (1988), *Employment Outlook, September 1988*, Paris, based on Chart 5.1, and OECD (1989), *Employment Outlook, July 1989*, Statistical Annex, Tables D and F.

se), or against the female share of employment across OECD countries as a whole, or against other occupations that are typically described as "feminised". Which is the appropriate indicator of feminisation depends on the point at issue, though these differences suggest that the term is often loosely applied. Table 5 permits certain of these comparisons to be made by showing trends in female labour market participation rates and the proportion of women in employment in OECD countries.

Women predominate in kindergartens

Table 4 shows clearly that women predominate in the pre-primary sector. This is a sector, as already seen, that is more or less integrated into the school system: in some countries, it is a full part, in others, it has a different tradition and even administrative responsibility from schools. It is arguable, in the latter case, whether the pre-primary sector should be included in deciding whether teaching is feminised since, strictly speaking, these personnel are not actually counted as teachers at all. Nevertheless, a common pattern is for 19 or more out of every 20 staff at this level to be a woman. *Greece* and the *United Kingdom* even report an entirely female kindergarten personnel, while the *Irish* case shows that exceptions to the rule are possible though women still well outnumber men even here.

Primary teaching is a feminised job

Evidence concerning teachers in primary schools is not subject to the same definitional ambiguities nor are the statistics ambiguous in the main message they purvey: primary school teaching is a feminised job. Typically, 7 or 8 out of every 10 primary school teachers are women. In *Italy*, the proportion comes close to 9 out of every 10. But even at this level of teaching, it is easy for the generalisations to smooth out the wrinkles of cross-country evidence. In *Japan* and *Norway*, 4 out of every 10 primary school teachers are men, while in *Greece* and *Turkey*, women are actually in a minority among the primary school staffs. The label "feminised" is less obviously applicable in these cases.

Though the highly skewed distribution of the sexes in leadership posts in schools is discussed separately below, that discussion can be anticipated at this point to provide an important qualification to the general picture provided by these aggregate statistics. The broad pattern of women comprising approximately three-quarters of primary school teachers underestimates the degree to which *classroom* teaching at this level is a women's job since the relatively few men who make up the other quarter or so include a high proportion who are already in leadership positions, many of whom will have a reduced or even negligible teaching load. It is necessary to bear in mind too that Table 4 refers indiscriminately to full- and part-time teachers in most cases, not to "full-time equivalents". Insofar as women are the majority among part-time staff, then two additional caveats to the general patterns revealed by these aggregate figures should be entered. First, these figures overestimate to a moderate degree the extent of feminisation if account is taken of total hours worked rather than aggregate numbers, counting full- and part-time teachers equally. Second, they underestimate to a varying degree the extent to which classroom teaching is a women's domain since a female preponderance in part-time teaching reinforces the distinction within the primary sector of male staff destined for leadership roles, on the one hand, and female staff making up the overwhelming majority of classroom teachers, on the other.

31

Sketchy evidence does indeed suggest that women are the majority, even in some cases the large majority, among part-time teachers at this level. They were two-thirds of the primary teachers on less than full-time schedules in *Japan* (66.8 per cent in 1987)[43], 9 out of 10 in the *Netherlands* in 1980[44], rising to as high as 98.2 per cent in *New Zealand* in 1986[45]. In *Sweden*, 84 per cent of over 32 000 primary and lower secondary school teachers who were either part-time or on partial leave from teaching duties were women in 1985[46]. How important the part-time factor is in absolute terms also varies widely across Member countries. Taking primary teachers, for example, the proportion counted as part-time varies from the negligible (in countries such as *Ireland, Japan*, and *Yugoslavia*), to approximately 10-15 per cent (*Austria, Belgium, Canada,* the *United Kingdom*), to as high as a third of all teachers at this level (the *Netherlands, Norway*)[47].

Women not clearly predominant in secondary education

In turning to teachers in secondary education, the situation becomes more complex and the label "feminised" sometimes inappropriate. For here, as Table 4 shows (albeit on the basis of incomplete information), there are decidedly fewer women in relative terms. At one end of the spectrum, to be sure, are some countries where women comprise the majority of secondary school staff as well; *Italy* is the clearest example from those covered in the table, with women making up two-thirds of lower secondary school teaching staff and over 62 per cent in the upper secondary general programmes. Women outnumber male teachers in lower secondary schools in *Austria, Denmark, France, Greece, Spain,* the *United Kingdom* and *Yugoslavia*, and, apart from Italy, in upper secondary general programmes only in *Austria, Spain*, and the *United Kingdom*. Elsewhere, for countries for which data are available in the table, women make up less than half of these teachers, though in many cases, the balance between the sexes remains a fairly even one.

One additional if approximate criterion for deciding whether the statistics for women secondary school teachers represent evidence of feminisation is to compare the percentages in Table 4 with those in Table 5, that show the proportion of women overall in the labour forces of OECD countries. Particularly at the upper secondary school level, there is little clear evidence of the relative presence of women standing significantly above women's share of employment overall. It cannot but be noticed that the higher the prestige of the particular educational level and the age of the students in question, with upper secondary general programmes at the upper end of the spectrum and primary and pre-primary at the lower, the greater is the proportion of men.

Other country data help complete some of the gaps of Table 4. *Swedish* figures underline the difference in female representation in the lower and upper reaches of the school system: women were over two-thirds of primary and lower secondary teachers in 1985 (68 per cent) but this falls to 44 per cent in the upper secondary programmes in that year[46]. In this case, it should be noted, however, that "upper secondary" covers both general and technical/vocational streams. In the latter programmes, the representation of women tends to fall further still, adding further nuance to the blanket description "feminised". Such differences can be seen in *Austria*, for example, where women are the majority in the teaching staffs of lower secondary and the academic secondary schools but were only 42.2 per cent in the vocational establishments (middle and higher schools)[6]. The comparable *Greek* figure of per cent female share in general secondary schools contrasts with 35 per cent in technical and vocational programmes[48]. The gap in the *French* case is of a comparable order: women are nearly 6 out of 10 of *lycée* teachers (59.6 per cent in

1986/87) and are only slightly less represented among the general lower secondary (*collège*) teaching staff (57.9 per cent) while making up 41.6 per cent of the LEP teachers (*lycée d'enseignement professionnel*, technical and professional upper secondary schools)[49]. And only a third of *Spanish* vocational education teachers were women in the same year in contrast with significantly higher percentages in the general branches of secondary education[50].

As usual, these generalities admit exceptions whether concerning the pattern for male teachers to be present in relatively higher numbers in the upper reaches of the school system or in vocational education. Two national exceptions are perhaps as striking for the contrast they provide between themselves as for the fact that they represent exceptions to the general tendencies. On the one hand there is *Finland* where women are practically as well represented in the ordinary (unpromoted) teaching staff at upper as in lower secondary education: 63.8 per cent of the former standing at an almost equal level (64.9 per cent) in the latter in 1984. Since the equivalent percentage in primary schools is 63 per cent, Finland is one of the few countries where teaching is feminised and where this applies evenly across the whole school system[51]. It is not an exception to another general rule, however, namely the very marked under-representation of women among school principals (see below). The *Netherlands* (the other example) shares with Finland a degree of non-conformity to the general patterns, in this case to the norm of there being more women teachers in general than in vocational education. Women were actually a slightly higher proportion among Dutch teaching staffs in junior and senior vocational education, compared with general secondary schools in 1985. The marked contrast with Finland, however, is in the actual percentages involved: for the schools in question, women were only 29 and 27 per cent of teaching staff respectively[44].

Towards greater feminisation?

Theoretical arguments can be deployed either to suggest that the numerical presence of women in teaching should have been expected to rise or to have fallen over recent years. Plausible reasons to expect growing feminisation would include the argument that where the relative attractiveness of teaching has declined, this should have resulted in a loss of men, given their typically privileged access to advantaged labour market slots, so leaving more openings to be filled by women. The lower likelihood than before of women leaving teaching (and other jobs) for family reasons could be expected to increase their presence on school staffs. The general point is that the growing female labour force participation rates should have resulted, other things being equal, in teaching, like other occupations, employing more women relative to men. (Table 5 shows just how significant that growth of participation in most OECD countries has been).

The arguments on the other side predicting decreasing "feminisation" include the proposition that, at least while difficult employment conditions for graduates prevailed, men who otherwise might have chosen another occupation or who might have left teaching instead stayed in education. It could also be argued, as is being heard as a source of concern particularly in North America, that women's labour market behaviour is becoming increasingly similar to that of men; just as many well qualified men have looked elsewhere and chosen alternative professions in the past, then so would women now tend to do the same.

a) No clear trend to feminisation in some countries

Actual trends are as mixed as these divergent arguments. The strength and applicability of the different pressures vary in each country depending both on the particular situation and status of teaching there and on the varying impact of the wide range of the other social and economic forces at play. In assessing trends, it matters too, of course, how long is the time span under consideration. One country where the statistics allow a relatively long-term view, the *United States*, has experienced a highly stable balance of approximately two-thirds female to one-third male teachers in public elementary and secondary schools since the early 1960s (women were 68.7 per cent in 1961, 65.7 per cent in 1971, 66.9 per cent in 1981, and 68.8 per cent in 1986)[28]. The same statistic for *Canada* showed a slight *fall* rather than a growing proportion of women in teaching over the decade from the school year 1973/74 (58 per cent dropping slightly to 56 per cent ten years later)[52]. In all schools in *Australia*, the female share of teaching posts remained very stable over the period 1976/88 (60 per cent and 59 per cent) as it has in secondary schools taken separately (46 per cent compared with 48 per cent)[53].

The *Netherlands* is another country which has not experienced a clear tendency for the share of women among teaching staff to rise. With pre-primary and primary taken together, this proportion rose only from 61 to 65 per cent over the 15 years after 1970, while at the secondary level the increase was a mere 2 percentage points from 26 to 28 per cent over the same period[44]. In vocational education and training, at the lower and upper secondary levels, the percentage of female teachers actually fell from 31 to 29 during this time, having gone up from 22 to 27 per cent in the corresponding general branches. A further example of stability rather than growing feminisation is seen in the sex ratio of primary school teachers in *Greece* which has remained at between 47 and 48 per cent women over the 15-year period up to the mid-1980s[48].

Among *Japanese* teachers too, the trends are not markedly upward. The female share at the primary level has risen a modest extent from approximately a half at the beginning of the 1970s to 56.5 per cent by 1987, though over the longer term, growing feminisation can be discerned since this proportion stood at approximately 45 per cent in the late 1950s and early 1960s. In lower secondary schools, the trend is somewhat more distinct since the female share in this case has risen from approximately a quarter to a third of teaching staff since the 1960s. (Comparatively, these levels are still low). Yet in the prestigious upper secondary schools, scarcely any change has been seen in this regard with women comprising a fairly constant 17 per cent of teachers throughout the period between 1955 and 1980, and they were still less than 1 teacher in 5 by 1987[31].

b) Growing proportions of female teachers

Elsewhere feminisation is clearer, though in a number of countries the main shifts towards more women teachers occurred in the late 1960s and early 1970s rather than recently. In schools other than at the primary level in *Greece*, for example, women are a growing presence on school staffs. This is rather less marked in general secondary schools (48.7 per cent women teachers in 1970/71, 53.2 in 1975/76, 55.3 in 1980/81, and 56.4 per cent in 1984/85), than in the technical and vocational schools with the biggest increases happening during the 1980s. The female share of teaching posts in these schools jumped from 22.8 in 1980/81 to 35.0 per cent in 1984/85 less than five years later, having stood at only 14.5 per cent at the beginning of the 1970s. Similar sharp increases have occurred in all school types in *Austria* as well. Taking the mid-1960s (1965) as the point of comparison with 1987, the corresponding percentages were: in primary schools, 57.4 and 80.6; in lower secondary schools, 48.8 and 60.5; in academic secondary schools, 36.6 and 53.3; in vocational middle and higher schools, 30 to 42.2 per cent. There is no doubt about the trend here.

New Zealand, Swedish, and United Kingdom data follow the same pattern if on a more moderate scale. Among *New Zealand* primary school teachers, the female share rose from 60.6 per cent in the mid-1960s (1965) to 68.1 by the beginning of the 1980s, and further still to 72.6 by 1986 while in lower secondary schools a stable balance at just under 40 per cent between the mid-1960s and mid-1970s had risen to 46.4 by the beginning of the 1980s and women had crossed from numerical minority to a slight majority by 1986. The increased presence of women among *Swedish* compulsory school teachers occurred dramatically at the end of the 1960s from 44 per cent in 1965 rising very sharply by over 20 percentage points to 65 per cent five years later, though the continuing rise has been very gradual since then (attaining 68 per cent in 1985). At the upper secondary level, less marked change has been witnessed and the corresponding percentages for the beginning and end points of the period between the mid-1960s and mid-1980s were 37 and 44. The gap in the proportion of women teachers between the primary and secondary levels remains a wide one in the *United Kingdom*, but in both sectors the trend over time has been firmly upward. Having been almost three-quarters (73.8 per cent) of primary teachers in the mid-1960s, women made up nearly 80 per cent by 1986/87, while in secondary schools they are still the minority (the percentages for 1965/66 and 1986/87 were 41.2 and 46.2).

As with the blanket descriptions of teachers in OECD countries as "ageing" (implying middle-aged) or as an already feminised profession, the assumption that women, proportionally, are swelling the profession in ever-growing numbers must, therefore, be treated with some care. In certain countries and at certain levels, there are discernible trends, while in others the main changes took place two decades ago, and in other countries again there is actually little firm evidence of an altering balance of the sexes in the teaching profession over time.

Women as principals

The position of women in the leadership posts (indicated here by access to principalships) in schools can be summarised briefly and generally: women are very markedly underrepresented as principals in all OECD countries. Although they are often the large majority of staff, few of them advance to become the principal or vice-principal of their school. The main exception to this generalisation is at the pre-primary level which is, as we have seen, a predominantly female domain in all countries, and even this exception itself admits exceptions; slightly fewer than half the kindergarten principals in *Japan* were women in 1987 (47.9 per cent), though they were nearly 9 out of every 10 of the corresponding vice-principals (88.2 per cent). Apart from the pre-primary sector, therefore, the general rule stands. Where there are differences on this count between OECD countries they are to be seen in terms of whether the female absence from the top jobs of teaching has softened over recent years or else is becoming still worse. Contrary to the expectation of an improvement, based on the generally improving female position in the professions, there has actually been a deterioration in some OECD countries of the situation of women in those leadership posts that represent career advancement from the classroom into positions of authority and administration. Such deterioration is a matter of urgency both from the viewpoint of equal rights and opportunities and because of the looming problem of future supply. Reversing the downward trend is one component of policies directed specifically at improving the attractiveness of teaching for women and, more generally, at meeting shortages as and when they arise.

Some figures readily illustrate the degree of female absence from teaching's top jobs while showing too the wide degree of variation from one country to another. For *primary* schools, illustrative percentages of female principals are: *Australia*, 41.2 (1988); *Finland*, 6.2 (1984); *France*, 44.9 (1985/86); *Japan*, 2.5 (1987); the *Netherlands*, 3 (1980) and 13 for pre-primary and primary together in 1985; *New Zealand*, 15.9 (1986); for all compulsory schools, *Denmark*, 7 (1988) and *Sweden*, 9 (1985).

At the *secondary* level, for some countries the figures are lower still while in others (contrary to what might be expected given the lower presence of women on secondary school staffs), there is actually a higher female proportion of heads than in primary schools. The figures for *Austria* are: compulsory secondary schools, 13.1 per cent; academic schools, 16.9 per cent of principals are female, while on the vocational side in technical institutions, 2.0 per cent; business colleges, 8.6 per cent; in domestic science and commercial schools, 51 per cent (1988). In *Finland*, corresponding percentages are 19.9 in lower secondary while in upper secondary schools, it stood at 15.1 in 1984. It is interesting to note that there are relatively fewer female principals in the lower than in the upper secondary schools in *Austria* while in *Finland* figures of between 15 and 20 per cent at these levels contrast with fewer than 1 principal in 20 being a women in primary schools there. Similarly in *Denmark*, there was a higher female share of headships at the upper secondary level (9 per cent) than at the primary and lower secondary levels (7 per cent) in 1988. The linear patterns of female over- and under-representation among teaching staffs as a whole do not apply neatly, therefore, to leadership posts. The corresponding *Japanese* figures are comparatively very low, though again a linear pattern is not in evidence – there was a greater (albeit very low) proportion of female principals at the upper secondary level (2.4 per cent) than in lower secondary schools where it stood at a mere 0.4 per cent in 1987.

Other national examples underline the point that everywhere women are very significantly under-represented as principals, that the patterns are not linear, and sizeable cross-country differences are to be found. The *Netherlands* can be contrasted with the Austrian case cited above (where the vocational sector in particular is a male domain) for in the former country there were still fewer women principals in general secondary schools (2 per cent in 1985) compared with 1 in 10 in junior and senior vocational schools. There are relatively more female principals than this in *New Zealand*, the proportion having stood at 15.8 per cent in 1986, while *Swedish* data also reinforce the unexpected result that the chances of women rising to the status of school principal can be greater in upper secondary schools than lower down in the system. The 9 per cent for compulsory school heads compares with 17 per cent at the upper secondary level in 1985. Since those chances should in theory be calculated from the base line of the numbers of female teachers at each level, even a small percentage advantage for women at the higher reaches of the system represents a significant step in chances of getting to the top.

Trends

Countries divide in terms of whether the marked female under-representation in principalships is actually becoming better or worse. Contrary to the common impression that improvements in the position of women in the labour market, however modest they may be in some cases, have been felt in every professional sphere, teaching is a case where, in some OECD countries at least, the promotion chances for women have actually deteriorated.

a) A deteriorating position for women principals in some countries

Canadian figures reveal just this trend. Such a decline can be explained in terms of a wide variety of factors: the varying fortunes of the primary and the secondary sectors in terms of trends in numbers of schools and students, school closure policies and the average size of schools (women are especially absent from headships of large secondary schools), the spread of co-education and the removal thereby of the girls' schools which have traditionally been an important avenue of promotion for female staff. These are in addition to the more direct factors of discriminatory selection practices, on the one hand, and the nature of women's professional ambitions, on the other. Of all these factors, the Canadian statistical report singles out declining enrolments for emphasis:

"Declining enrolments have resulted in a subsequent decline in the number of positions in school administration (principals, vice-principals, and department heads). The number of these positions dropped by 1% but the number of women in the positions had declined by 19% [between 1972/73 and 1983/84]. In 1972/73, 17% of all school principals were women; in 1983/84, they accounted for 14%. The majority of women principals (94%) are employed at the elementary level where they represent 16% of principals. Women make up 5% of secondary school principals"[54].

Evidence from Australia and the Netherlands points to a similar decline. Sampson's summary of the *Australian* situation[55] includes such telling facts as that in Victoria between 1971 and 1983, the proportion of female secondary heads was nearly halved from 1 in 5 to 11 per cent only. More recent data suggest, however, that this deterioration may have been halted: the Australian Teachers' Federation 1988 survey of government schools found levels of 17 per cent female principalships and 32 per cent of women in promoted posts – an improvement over the 1986 situation and still more over 1984[56]. The *Netherlands*, a country which has comparatively low levels of women both in teaching and in the labour market generally, has also witnessed a declining proportion of women in headship positions: in preprimary and primary schools taken together, it fell from half in 1980 to 36 per cent in 1985 (and within this sector, taking only primary schools, the 1970s saw the percentage of women heads drop from an already low 6 to a mere 3 per cent by the end of the decade). Between the mid-1970s and mid-1980s, the signs of deterioration in this regard have been just as evident in secondary education: from a quarter of principalships in vocational establishments, the female share dropped markedly over this period to only 1 in 10 by 1985, while in general schools the corresponding decline was from 4 per cent to a lowly 2 per cent by 1985.

b) Mixed trends

Even *Sweden*, a country with exceptionally high female labour market participation rates and a long-standing tradition of anti-discrimination legislation, provides a mixed picture rather than one of unqualified improvement. For whereas the proportion of female headships in compulsory schools has risen from 4 to 9 per cent since the beginning of the 1970s, the 1965 level was actually higher still than that for 1985 at 1 woman principal in 10. The situation in upper secondary education is not ambiguous, however, and here there has been clear improvement; from a low 4 per cent in the mid-1960s, the presence of women in principals' posts had grown and stood at 17 per cent two decades later. *Austrian* figures reveal mixed trends too. While the position of women has strongly and rapidly improved since the beginning of the 1980s in primary schools (27.6 per cent of heads in 1980 rising sharply to 41.2 by 1988), in the other types of schools, the corresponding figures have either

37

been stable or else have even declined. Even in domestic science and commercial schools – a traditional female stronghold – the share of women heads has fallen from two-thirds to a half since the beginning of the 1980s.

c) More women heads

Only in Finland and New Zealand, among the OECD countries for which trends data were available to the author, are consistent increases apparent and in the *Finnish case* such increases are small (though the time span 1980/84 is also too short for the establishment of clear trends). In these two years, the appropriate proportions were: primary, 4.3 and 6.2 per cent; lower secondary, 18.8 and 19.9 per cent; upper secondary 14.7 and 15.1 per cent. For *New Zealand*, a stronger increase can be discerned: in only the six years that elapsed after 1980, the proportion of female principals in primary schools had gone up from 5.6 to 15.9 per cent, and in lower secondary schools, the increase was from 10.5 to 15.8 per cent. Perhaps from the standpoint of women teachers in New Zealand this may appear as only modest improvement, but from a cross-national perspective it is one of the few examples of clear improvement in the representation of women as heads of schools among OECD countries.

*

* *

To sum up, from the different facts and developments outlined in this chapter, it is clear that the situation of teachers, even in terms of the limited number of dimensions discussed above, differ across countries. Generalisations that are meant to apply to all national situations must certainly be treated with caution. Some facts or trends, such as the substantial under-representation of women in leadership posts, are universal but even then there are wide cross-country differences and divergent trends. This chapter has shown too that caution should be exercised concerning certain of the common labels and stereotypes that attach to teachers and teaching. The data show that teacher numbers have tended not to decline, that only teaching at certain levels can be properly described as "feminised", and that common evocation of the ageing factor may often be exaggerated. But the chapter was also careful to point out that while expressions of disquiet about the *past* and the *contemporary* situation may sometimes be subject to journalistic exaggeration, common labels may prove increasingly apt in the *future*. In this regard, the impact of increasing numbers of retiring teachers and the unequal promotion prospects between men and women are areas for particular concern.

NOTES AND REFERENCES

1. In particular, the periodic joint ILO/UNESCO reviews of teacher status and working conditions to assess the application of the 1966 Recommendation on the Status of Teachers. The most recent is the ILO (1989) "Joint ILO-UNESCO Committee of Experts on the Application of the Recommendation concerning the Status of Teachers", Geneva. The previous review was ILO (1981), *Employment and Working Conditions of Teachers*, Geneva. See also the joint EEC/Netherlands study on the conditions of service of teachers in the European Community carried out by the Stichting Research Group in the Netherlands: ECSC-EEC-EAEC (1988), *The Conditions of Service of Teachers in the European Community*, Brussels and Luxembourg.

2. A special meeting of OECD national correspondents and experts on education statistics (convened in June 1988) discussed the difficulties and complexities of international comparisons in this field concluding that substantially greater work using national definitions and statistics would be needed as a prerequisite for such comparisons.

3. Examples taken from the national reports by Besnard, V. and Burger, K. (1987), "Teachers in the Netherlands" (OECD working document, English text only), p. 10 and by Könnöla, J. and Merilainen, K. (1988), "Teachers in Finland" (OECD working document), p. 25.

4. Spyropoulos, G.P. (1988), "La formation des enseignants en Grèce" (OECD working document, French text only), Table I.

5. Burke, G. (1989), "Teachers in Australia: Teacher Supply and Teacher Quality: Social and Economic Aspects" (OECD working document), Table 1.

6. Paseka, A. (1988), "Teachers in Austria: The Situation of Women Teachers in the Austrian Education System" (OECD working document), Table 1.

7. Rasmussen, T.K. (1988), "Teachers in Denmark" (OECD working document), p. 3.

8. Ministère de l'Education Nationale (1988), *Repères et références statistiques sur les enseignements et la formation: édition 1988*. Direction de l'évaluation et de la prospective, sous-direction des enquêtes statistiques et des études, Vanves, pp. 71 and 83.

9. U.S. Department of Education (1988), *The Digest of Education Statistics: 1988 Edition*, National Center for Education Statistics, Washington D.C., Table 51.

10. Statistics Canada (1985), *Salaries and Qualifications of Teachers in Public Elementary and Secondary Schools 1983-84*, Ottawa, Table 4.

11. Department of Education and Science (1989), *Education Statistics for the United Kingdom: 1988 Edition*, Statistical Bulletin 1/89, Table 8.

12. Ministry of Education, Science, and Culture (1988), *Statistical Abstract of Education, Science and Culture: 1988 Edition* (English version), Tokyo, pp. 31, 34, 38, 46.

13. Federal Ministry of Education and Science (1986), *Basic and Structural Data 1986-87 Edition* (English version), Bonn, p. 36 and *ibid* (1988), pp. 48-49.

14. U.S. Department of Education (1988), *op. cit.*, Table 51.

15. Federal Ministry of Education and Science (1986), *op. cit.*, p. 37. The 1988-1989 edition does not present the data comparably but these data show that, over the following two years to 1987 pupil/teacher ratios have in general continued to fall, though they have stabilised for primary

schools and have actually risen in the pre-primary sector. (Federal Ministry of Education and Science (1988), *op. cit.*, pp. 46-47).

16. Spyropoulos, G.P. (1988), *op. cit.*, Table II.
17. Rasmussen, T.K. (1988), *op. cit.*, p. 3.
18. Besnard, V. and Burger, K. (1988), *op. cit.*, p. 5.
19. Burke, G. (1989), *op. cit.*, Table 4.
20. Department of Education and Science (1989), *Education Statistics for the United Kingdom: 1988 Edition*, Statistical Bulletin ¹/₈, Table 1. The PTR for secondary education excludes upper secondary level education provided in non-advanced further education colleges.
21. Angrén, B., Lovgren, E., and Skog-Ostlin K. (1987), "Teachers in Sweden" (OECD working document), p. 7.
22. Department of Employment, Education, and Training (1987), *Schooling in Australia: Statistical Profile No. 1*, Canberra, Table 3.3.
23. Information communicated to the Secretariat by the Italian national authorities.
24. Discussed in OECD/CERI reports: OECD/CERI (1981), *The Education of the Handicapped – Integration in the School*, Paris and (1985), *Integration of the Handicapped in Secondary Schools*. For a specific discussion of the implications for teachers see Woolfson, R. (1987), "Integration of the Handicapped in Schools and its Implications for Teachers: Lessons from Research" (OECD working document).
25. "Les enseignants en Italie: Statut social et problèmes soulevés par l'exercice de la profession" (1987) (OECD working document, French text only), p. 7.
26. Jordell, K. O. (1989), "Teachers in Norway" (OECD working document), pp. 1-2.
27. Statistics Canada (1985), *op. cit.*, Table 2.
28. U.S. Department of Education (1988), *op. cit.*, Table 54.
29. Paseka, A. (1988), *op. cit.*, pp. 3-5.
30. Burke, G. (1989), *op. cit.*, Table 8.
31. Ministry of Education, Science, and Culture (1988), *op. cit.*, p. 35, 38, and 46.
32. *Education Statistics for the United Kingdom 1980 and 1986 editions*, HMSO, Table 20 (1980), Table 10 (1986).
33. Ministère de l'Education Nationale (1986), *Le personnel enseignant des établissements publics du second degré - données par âge - 1984-85*, Note d'information No. 86-13, SPRESE, Vanves.
34. Ministère de l'Education nationale (1988), *op. cit.*, p. 69.
35. England and Wales country statement for the "International Conference on Teacher Training for Basic Education" held in Novi Sad, Yugoslavia, 3-5 October, 1988 (OECD working document).
36. Lesourne, J. (1988), *Education et Société Demain: à la recherche des vraies questions*, Ministère de l'Education Nationale, Editions La Découverte et Journal *Le Monde*, Paris. The relevant chapter of the technical annex to this report is reproduced in "Les enseignants en France" (OECD working document, French text only), 1988.
37. Besnard, V. and Burger, K. (1987), *op. cit.*, p. 5.
38. Rasmussen, T. K. (1988), *op. cit.*, p. 15.
39. Jeuthe, E. (1989), "Teachers in Germany: The Employment of Teachers against the Background of Teacher Surplus, the Ageing of the Profession, and a Decline in Student Numbers" (OECD working document), p. 5.
40. OECD (1989), "OECD Review of Ireland: Background Report". A review of the Irish Education System prepared by the Department of Education, Dublin (Document on General Distribution).

41. Spyropoulos, G.P. (1988), *op. cit.*, p. 13 and Table III.

42. See, for example, Lortie, D. (1975), *School Teacher: A Sociological Study*, University of Chicago Press, Chicago.

43. Ministry of Education, Science, and Culture (1988), *op. cit.*, p. 34.

44. Netherlands correspondence with the Secretariat on the position of women in teaching (Netherlands reply on women teachers).

45. New Zealand reply on women teachers.

46. Swedish reply on women teachers.

47. See OECD (1989), *Education in OECD Countries 1986-87: A Compendium of Statistical Information*, Paris, Table 2.2.

48. Spyropoulos, G.P. (1988), *op. cit.*, Table IV.

49. Ministère de l'Education nationale (1988), *op. cit.*, p. 77.

50. Gonzalez Dorrego, B.G. (1988), "Les Enseignants en Espagne" (OECD working document, French text only), p. 17.

51. Könnöla, J. and Merilainen, K. (1988), *op. cit.* Table 1.

52. Statistics Canada (1985), *Education in Canada 1983-84 edition*, Ottawa, Chart 23.

53. Burke, G. (1989), *op. cit.*, Table 6.

54. Statistics Canada (1985), *Salaries and Qualifications of Teachers in Elementary and Secondary Schools*, *op. cit.*, p. 12. See also Porat, K.L. (1985), "The Woman in the Principal's Chair in Canada", *Phi Delta Kappan*, December.

55. Sampson, S. N. (1987), "Equal Opportunity, alone, is not enough or Why there are More Male Principals in Schools these Days", *Australian Journal of Education*, Vol. 31, No. 1.

56. Burke, G. (1989), *op. cit.*, p. 7.

Chapter 3

TEACHING AS A PROFESSION: ITS ATTRACTIVENESS AND THE ISSUE OF SUPPLY

INTRODUCTION

The distinctions and differences that were underlined in the previous chapter – such as between teachers in pre-primary and primary and in secondary schools, between general and vocational streams, between lower and upper secondary branches, between unpromoted classroom teachers and principals, between men and women – provide a useful introduction to this one. They qualify descriptions of the status and situation of teachers as if they were unitary and shared by all. The situation of the pre-primary assistant – typically young, female, and often poorly paid – is, in many respects, worlds apart from the upper secondary pre-university subject specialist. That heterogeneity among teachers is an important characteristic of the profession within a single country while countries differ too in the degree to which teaching overall is largely unified or else more nearly resembles a series of interlocking occupations.

The aim of the early sections of this chapter is to discuss various aspects of the professional character of the occupation and activity of teaching, seeking to distinguish between normative and descriptive definitions, between different conceptions of teacher work and status, and between the exercise of identifying telling factors influencing that status and the perennial debate in some countries about characteristics and membership of "true" professions. The chapter then goes on to discuss the closely related aims of improving the attractiveness of teaching and of maintaining and increasing teacher supply, with reference to concrete trends and examples. It eschews a detailed forecasting of future supply and demand in favour of the delineation of a number of key developments that may induce very serious problems of shortages over the decade ahead without effective counteractive measures. Special attention is given to the position of teachers in vocational education and training.

THE PROFESSIONAL NATURE OF TEACHING

Divergent conceptions of the teacher's task

Is teaching a profession? Few teachers hesitate in answering this question in the affirmative. Their sense of membership is reflected in the common label "the teaching

43

profession". Outside their ranks, the response is less unanimous; their professional status is not necessarily recognised in full either by the public at large or by potential entrants. Teachers themselves complain often that the recognition they receive does not match the demands of the work. The contentious nature of teachers' professional standing is indicated by the voluminous literature addressing the very question that introduces this paragraph. One prominent contribution to that literature even refers to teachers as one of the "semi-professions" [1]. The ambiguity is amplified when the perspective is cross-national. The very term carries a specific meaning in English, as Perkin[2] underlines in the quotation reproduced later in this section. It is essential, in clarifying the variety of claims and assertions, to distinguish the *descriptive* exercise of detailing the occupational characteristics, recognition, and rewards that teachers display and receive compared with others from the essentially *normative* one of proposing how these should be ideally organised. Teachers may well agree as a matter of fact that they do not receive sufficient recognition in the form of full professional status; the normative claim in contrast may well be for this to be rectified.

The concept of "open professionalism" for teachers which was developed within the OECD work in the 1970s provided a good illustrative example of the distinction between the normative and the descriptive. It lists defining characteristics of what teaching ought to be and why this is a desirable path of development for education policies in general. It remains a highly pertinent question to ask why, as a matter of fact, actual developments fall short of this guiding idea.

A highly summary statement of the notion of "open professionalism", focusing on departures from common practice rather than attempting a full definition of teacher duties and responsibilities, is:

"Teachers' duties and the relevant timetables should be compatible with the recent development of such tasks as:

i) Team-work with colleagues;
ii) Individual counselling for pupils;
iii) Contact with parents and the local community;
iv) In-service training;
v) Action research activities;
vi) Participation by teachers in the planning and management of the school or in expressing their views about the development of the education system as a whole.

So long as teachers are increasingly required to provide their pupils with an understanding of the concepts of responsibility and autonomy, it is difficult to see why they should be denied the opportunity of assuming their own responsibilities in this area and of effectively participating in the management of their schools and in the debate about general developments affecting the education system. Moreover, the individualisation of teaching which the teacher is called upon to introduce would need equally to be reflected in the attitude the administration adopts towards the teachers as individuals, with due regard to their reactions, aspirations and professional commitment"[3].

The concept "open professionalism" enshrines the idea that the modern teacher, at the focal point of rapidly changing and highly demanding educational policies, needs to be both open to communal influence and co-operation – with colleagues, the school, on-going research and developments, parents, the community – and to receive respect as an individual professional. Reconciling these two elements in practice may not, however, be straightforward. It would entail an openness to outside influence that enhances, not diminishes, the individual's sense of commitment and responsibility.

One reason why these can prove difficult to reconcile in practice is that there exist quite different conceptions of the nature of teaching held by the principal actors involved. Part of the process of forging the new consensus, as called for in Chapter 1, will lie precisely in the establishment of a greater measure of common understanding of what the role and duties of the modern teacher should be. Darling-Hammond *et al.*[4] have identified a useful four-way typology of conceptions of teacher work, distilled from opinions about, and policies towards, teachers:

- *Teaching as labour:* the activities of the teacher should be rationally planned, and programmatically organised by administrators, with the teacher merely responsible for carrying out the instructional programme;
- *Teaching as craft:* teaching is seen in this conception as requiring a répertoire of specialised techniques and as well as mastering the techniques, the teacher must acquire rules for their application;
- *Teaching as profession:* the teacher needs not only a répertoire of specialised techniques but also the ability to exercise judgement about when these techniques should be applied and hence a body of theoretical knowledge;
- *Teaching as art:* based not only on professional knowledge and skills but on a set of personal resources uniquely defined; techniques and their application may be novel, unconventional, and unpredictable.

These categories are useful and suggestive rather than definitive and they are also not mutually exclusive. One category might arguably apply more nearly to certain types of teachers than to others; conflicting claims will often be made by the same groups or individuals, whether teachers or others – to be like workers in some respects, and like professionals or artists in others. It should be underlined that these conceptions of teaching work are ideal types, not to be found in a pure form in the real world. But the way that politicians, administrators, and others regard teaching, and the way that they may want teachers to be appraised, can be closely related to different conceptions of the sort encapsulated by these four categories. Once again, the need is underlined to clarify and make explicit the underlying assumptions about "teacher work". Underlying many open disputes about teachers' salaries and conditions of service are covert disagreements between those who regard teaching as "labour" or "craft" and teachers who want to be treated as "professionals" or "artists"[5].

Clarification of roles and responsibilities needed rather than strict definitions of "professions" and "professionalism"

The wide differences between these conceptions underline that the problematic professional standing of teachers has an important political component and cannot be resolved as a technical, definitional matter. Clarification, and agreement where possible, of priorities and duties is a matter of urgency as argued above. Argument over whether teachers constitute a "true" profession, in contrast, can be a sterile exercise. Examination of the origins of the term "profession" provides valuable clues to the confusion that it has since engendered as a term; Perkin[2] has traced these origins to show how a "false dichotomy" has entered into modern thinking and vocabulary, certainly in the English language:

"The word 'profession' as now increasingly used in many languages for an especially desirable and dignified occupation with an implication of intellectual training and a largely mental exercise, is derived from a twist in Anglo-American usage in the late

18th and 19th centuries. Until then, even in the English-speaking countries, it still meant 'occupation' and no more, as is still normally the case with French *profession* and German *Beruf.* See for example the bracketing of pinmakers, weavers, merchants, bankers and insurance underwriters with clergymen, physicians and attorneys in Robert Campbell's *The London Tradesman* (1747), where the immense differences of status are measured by apprenticeship premiums and 'sums necessary to set up as master', not by length of training or supposed expertise, but without any dividing line between professions and the rest. A few occupations – the Anglican clergy but not dissenting ministers, barristers but not attorneys and solicitors, physicians but not surgeons and apothecaries – were known as 'learned' or 'liberal' professions... How and why the epithets 'learned' and 'liberal' fell out of use is something of a mystery....

This twist of usage created a false dichotomy for status-chasing occupations in the English-speaking world of the 19th century, which bequeathed it in turn to the sociologists and historians of the 20th. Instead of arranging occupations in a reasonably continuous hierarchy of remuneration and status... the terminology of professions suggested a clear-cut, black and white distinction between those occupations which could and those which could not claim professional status... This in turn led to a meretricious search for the defining traits or characteristics of the true profession and a vast sociological literature dedicated to the three, six or fourteen essential features which separated the ... noble professions from the common or garden occupations" (pp. 12-13).

The search for *the* defining qualities and membership of "the" profession is thus an exercise of interest for sociological comparisons of occupations, perhaps, but of limited practical value. Doctors and lawyers are the most frequently cited examples but how far membership is seen to extend beyond these two is less certain. Even these cited occupations differ from each other in crucial respects – the applicability of the notion of a vocational calling is not the same in each case and many practising lawyers are scarcely distinguishable, in attitude or training, from those in business and finance, who have often been so carefully excluded from the term "profession" in the past. How akin the essentially public service of teaching is to the private practice of certain professions is certainly open to debate. In some countries (the Scandinavian region offers good examples here), pay and conditions are set by close reference to other workers in the public sector. In certain OECD countries, teachers enjoy the title and tenure of public civil servants (as in, for example, Denmark, France, Germany, Greece, Italy, Luxembourg, Portugal, and Spain).

Not only is the concept "profession" an uncertain litmus against which to assess the condition and standing of the teaching force, but in many OECD countries that force is typified by internal divisions in their profiles, conditions, and prospects. One crucial disjuncture has already been described in detail in the previous chapter – that between women and men. While their formal opportunities may be commonly shared, their experienced career prospects are markedly divergent. There are also differences between types of teachers deriving from the level and setting in which they are located which, in turn, can vary significantly across countries. Recent educational policies have blurred certain of the sharper boundaries between these settings in some systems: pre-primary provision may be more closely integrated into the elementary cycle (for example, the Netherlands); primary and secondary schooling more closely combined to constitute the compulsory phase (Scandinavian countries); in a variety of countries, a heavier emphasis than in the past is placed on subject specialism in primary schools; a greater theoretical component introduced into technical and vocational programmes at the lower and upper secondary levels and corresponding (if less far-reaching) efforts to enhance awareness of the worlds of employment and work in academic streams[6]. Yet despite such signs of integration, very evident differences of approach and culture remain and these are reflected in turn in the teaching staff employed in each.

This is scarcely better illustrated than by the distinctive status enjoyed by the upper secondary teacher of academic subjects in the *Gymnasium* and *lycée* who frequently shares more in common with the university don than the elementary school teacher or the vocational workshop specialist. This is seen most starkly, perhaps, within OECD countries, in the German-speaking region. These tend to possess a highly distinct vocational sector and they maintain one of the widest demarcations between the background and qualifications of infant teachers, at one end of the spectrum, and those preparing students for university study, at the other. The preparation of personnel for the pre-primary sector is still entrusted to the upper secondary level in Austria and Germany (and Italy), rather than to higher education as in many other OECD countries. In contrast, the norm for the preparation of teachers for students at the upper secondary level is at the elevated level of the *Magister* or doctoral study in Austria and Switzerland[7].

The special case of vocational education

Developments concerning teachers in the vocational sector amply illustrate the difficulty of addressing all teachers as a single professional body. These developments also raise the question of the socialisation into work that different teachers receive – what are the consequences of the different routes into, and training requirements imposed on, those in vocational education compared with their general colleagues? In most OECD countries, greater priority has come to be assigned to the technical and vocational sector and a realisation that existing gulfs between the cultures of "education" and "training" may be highly counterproductive to students, teachers, and to the provision of learning opportunities adaptable to the needs of all. The question of the adequacy of traditional sources of recruitment and methods of training for the teachers in vocational education for the provision of high quality and flexible programmes thus becomes a matter of urgency.

In some systems, particularly in Europe – Austria, Belgium, France, Germany, Ireland, Luxembourg, the Netherlands, Switzerland are prime examples – there has long existed a very distinct institutional base for vocational training within the school system. In others, there are separate vocational tracks within a common institutional setting (senior high schools in the United States, for example, have "college", "vocational" and "general" curricular programmes). Or, the new priority accorded to technical and vocational education may have resulted in the creation of distinct programmes such as in the United Kingdom – in this case, either in schools with the recent widespread adoption of the Technical and Vocational Education Initiative (TVEI) or involving co-operation between training agencies, employers, and schools and colleges [the Youth Training Scheme (YTS)] though organisation and levels of financial support are subject to constant change. In many countries, especially where there is a well-established tradition of vocational education, there are separate training requirements for teachers of these programmes. In Norway, for example, upper secondary teachers come in by quite different routes, either through general training at a university (41 per cent), or in a higher teacher training college for vocational education (ENSFPEP) (34 per cent), or in regional colleges for specialist vocational fields (25 per cent)[8]. Vocational teachers in Ireland are actually employed by a different authority at the national rather than the local level, in this case by a state Vocational Education

47

Council, not a school management board as are other teachers[9]. Vocational and technical subject teachers often possess a distinct ethos and background, more closely allied to the industrial and commercial fields from which they come and prepare students for than to their general subject colleagues.

These developments give rise to some of the complex policy questions confronting both the education authorities and teachers as a body today. For the authorities, the aim of increasing the theoretical content of practical training in the face of the high skill demands and rapid changes of modern economies, combined with the pressure to greater standardization of entry of teachers for reasons of quality control and ensuring adequate pedagogical preparation, may risk jeopardising the very ethos of employment relevance and awareness that they are otherwise seeking to promote. Indeed, the OECD country with one of the most highly developed vocational sectors – Germany – has recently reversed the requirement of all teachers to possess a university qualification in order again to allow in a quota (20 per cent is the current aim) from the traditional vocational route through enterprises precisely to safeguard that distinct contact with the world of employment[9]. There are critical questions to be resolved about ensuring a high quality supply of teachers with the right mix of theoretical knowledge and practical know-how in fields where this combination of skills will frequently be at a premium in the labour market outside teaching. The emerging problem of shortages, discussed below, may be felt with special acuteness in these fields as overall labour shortages become more common in the decade ahead. This supply question arises repeatedly in the topics covered in the rest of the chapter; suffice it here to raise the issue of the possible room for conflict between the imposition of fixed standards of entry and training that may enhance the professional cohesiveness of teachers overall, on the one hand, and the search for flexible and up-to-date staff with "relevant" knowledge and experience, on the other.

For teachers, these developments in the vocational field may hold significant repercussions for the quest after enhanced professional status. A major factor impelling reform has been the clear trend for many more young people to stay in education and training than before. This has heralded the corresponding arrival of new groups of youngsters seeking a different diet of learning from traditional academic fare. All this has resulted in the burgeoning of programmes, some within the formal education system, others partially or wholly outside it. With such variety of provision for learning, both public and private, the term "the training market" has even been coined to describe the organisation of current provision[10]. In all this, the establishment and organisation of the programmes have tended to receive considerably more attention than the source, quality, and performance of the personnel that staff them. But the more the "training market" becomes an established feature of OECD systems, the more the professional backgrounds and characteristics of the teachers involved will come to the fore. Coming on top of a period when the teaching profession itself has sought upgrading through all-graduate entry, and the education authorities have often insisted on stricter entry requirements on the argument of safeguarding quality, the new expansion has brought with it the countervailing feature of the diversification of teaching personnel. We cannot say whether that in itself is a good or bad thing but it is an area that needs to be addressed; the traditional separation of vocational provision and its relative neglect in mainstream discussion cannot continue as before. Basic information, let alone research, on all these matters concerning the vocational sector and programmes remains weak. If these programmes are to attain the quality and importance held for them by official policy, the problem of the paucity of information needs to be rectified and the issues and problems confronting them need to be more widely addressed.

Factors affecting teachers' professional status

Since the defining nature of teachers' professional status is a matter of endless controversy, it follows that analysis of the factors making for change in that status can be no less open-ended. Still more does this apply when the focus is cross-national with the varying organisation, conditions, and levels of public recognition that this implies. The international perspective nevertheless permits attention to three broad factors with undoubted relevance for the status of the teaching force. One such factor has already been mentioned in Chapter 2 – *size*. In most OECD countries, there are simply too many teachers for high status to be automatically accorded in the public mind. That factor also significantly reduces the room for radical changes in economic awards in the short term when public expenditure is under severe constraint. But size is a limiting, not a determining condition; renewed priority for education, reinforced by perceptions of potential problems of teacher supply, can result in major efforts to enhance the attractiveness of the profession even if that implies greater expenditure. Nowhere are these different pressures better illustrated than in current debates in France. The proposition (at the time of writing) was to grant an extra FF 6 billion to education in 1989 as part of a total additional 54 billion over the next four years. Naturally, these sums are hailed by some as a just indication of the renewed priority accorded to education in general and teachers specifically, by others as scarcely likely to dent the poor image of the profession.

A second relevant factor to the changing status of teachers seen throughout the OECD family of countries is their *educational qualification levels*. The anomalous situation prevails that as the qualifications of teachers reach levels never before attained, so do complaints become more vocal – from teachers that the status of the profession is declining, from critics that schools and teachers are somehow failing. Not surprisingly, the result is a feeling of malaise. Yet, there is no doubt that the background qualifications of the teaching force are higher than ever. In a number of countries, teaching has become an all-graduate profession. More graduates with advanced university degrees now teach in classrooms than ever before. Reported levels of unqualified staff have been in long-term decline across OECD countries, though there remain significant pockets, even within systems enjoying relative surplus, of unqualified staff teaching shortage subjects or of qualified staff responsible for classes "out of position" from those that their original training prepared them for. And there are countries where unqualified staff remains a major problem. In Spain, for example, where university-level teacher training allows for six different specialisms, only in 41 per cent of posts are teachers matched to those subjects[11]. Portugal reports an identical proportion of 5th and 6th grade teachers as less than fully qualified, as in Spain[12].

The anomaly needs to be put in the broader context of the massive long-term expansion of higher education, combined with the reality that Neave has described starkly as: "the decade 1975-85 witnessed the whole-scale collapse of the major single employment sector of higher education, namely the education system itself."[13] Table 6 gives an indication of the extent to which higher education has now become the normal experience for a sizeable minority – and exceptionally, in the North American OECD countries, the majority – of each cohort of young people passing through the system. If the data permitted a longer historical perspective, the story of expansion would be still more dramatically told.

The coincidence of rising qualification levels and a decline in perceived standing thus receives partial explanation – graduate status is no longer an exceptional privilege. The popular perception of teachers in former times as guardians of wisdom is no longer assured when advanced knowledge has become the normal requirement of many occupations. Adapting Trow's three-way typology to refer not to higher education systems generally but

Table 6

PROPORTION (%) OF THE AGE GROUP IN THIRD LEVEL (HIGHER) EDUCATION:
A) NEW ENTRANTS FOR THE CORRESPONDING AGE GROUP: 1986
B) TOTAL ENROLMENTS AS A PROPORTION OF
THE 20-24 AGE GROUP: 1971, 1975, 1986

Country	(A)	(B)		
	1986	1971	1975	1986
Australia	38.8[a]	17.0	23.6	27.4[a]
Austria	21.8	12.7	18.6	27.3
Belgium	42.9	17.6	21.3	32.2
Canada	..	34.5	39.4	55.3
Denmark	36.5	21.4	29.4	28.9
Finland	41.6[b]	13.9	27.2	35.6
France	32.9	19.4	24.4	30.0
Germany	27.3	14.7	24.6	29.4
Greece	32.8	13.4	17.4	27.0
Ireland	27.6[a b]	13.7	19.2	24.6[a]
Italy	25.3	19.1	25.1	26.1[c]
Japan	35.8	..	..	29.6
Netherlands	30.3[a d]	20.9	25.5	31.4
New Zealand	37.6[e]	..	27.6	35.8
Norway	..	17.3	22.1	32.4
Portugal	14.4[a]	..	10.0	11.3[a]
Spain	30.4	9.8	21.0	30.2
Sweden	67.5	21.9	28.8	30.7
Switzerland	35.3[a]	11.2	14.1	21.2[a]
Turkey	12.2	..	9.1	9.8
United Kingdom	33.1	16.7	21.3	22.3
United States	64.4	49.3	57.3	60.2
Yugoslavia	29.2	..	..	19.0

a) 1985/86.
b) Full-time only.
c) 1984/85.
d) Universities only.
e) Excluding Technical Correspondence Institutes and Polytechnics/Technical Institutes.

Sources: A) OECD (1988), *Education in OECD Countries 1986-87: A Compendium of Statistical Information*, Paris, Table 3.2.
For definitions and coverage see source.
B) OECD educational and demographic data banks.

to the graduate emerging from them, he or she no longer belongs to the "elite" but to the "mass", and even approaching, in the North American cases, "universal" membership[14]. The market power of the credential, as well as the content of the qualification, change accordingly.

A third major factor affecting status to be singled out here has also already received considerable coverage in the previous chapter – *feminisation*. The rewards and status of teachers decline, it is commonly asserted, in direct proportion to the growing number and predominant place of women among their ranks. That assertion springs from diametrically opposite viewpoints: the sexist opinion that such an inverse correlation is a normal, even natural, labour market mechanism, on one side, or, conversely, the view that, as a matter of fact, "women's work" tends to be systematically undervalued. The evidence of occupational segregation and earnings differentials by sex corroborate the latter view[15]. So does the evidence of the difficult struggle of female workers and professionals to win practical results from the legal principle "equal pay, comparable worth"[16].

The difficulty with the "growing feminisation leads to declining status" thesis lies in establishing the direction of causality: is it the growing presence of women that leads to declining public recognition or, vice versa, does an existing drop in standing lead to "male flight"? Account needs also to be taken of the wide variability concerning female representation in teaching by level, across countries, and over time, as documented in Chapter 2. The correct view concerning the direction of causality is probably an interactive combination of the two factors outlined above. Incidental support for the notion that attractiveness of a profession is directly associated in the public mind with masculinity as a matter of fact, however awkward that conclusion may be, derives from the recent national publicity campaign in France to foster the overall image of teaching which chose prominently to display men rather than women. The implication, explicit or implicit, is that portraying a masculine image is to boost appeal.

The problematic status of teachers is thus affected by a number of general developments both within education, and in the broader context of the labour market, economy, and society of which we have singled out but three. In Chapter 1, attention was drawn to the temptation to romantic exaggeration that many accounts of past prestige fall into. To be sure, the rural headmasters – the "black hussards" of Jules Ferry's 3rd République in France – may well have enjoyed considerable respect as pillars of their communities. At the same time, however, many teachers were ill-formed assistants imparting a narrow curriculum to generations of youngsters, most of whom were destined to leave school at the earliest legal moment. And sociological studies of occupational prestige do allow comparisons over time that warn against simplistic theses of uninterrupted decline: for example, the public esteem accorded to public school teachers in the United States appears to have actually risen between just after World War II and 1963[17]. To repeat, care must be taken with exaggerated notions of the high levels of public prestige traditionally enjoyed by teachers.

The further point to be underscored here is that whether status has risen or fallen compared with a half century or more ago is not directly relevant to the dominant contemporary question of whether sufficient recognition and reward is accorded for the very high demands now made of the modern teacher, demands that, in all likelihood, will continue to increase in the future. Comparing professional demands, on one side, and professional rewards, on the other, requires attention, however, to the third element of the triad introduced in Chapter 1, namely professional competence and commitment – professionalism.

THE ATTRACTIVENESS OF TEACHING AND ENSURING ADEQUATE SUPPLY

Improving the attractiveness of the profession and ensuring teacher supply: two interlocking aims

It is natural that these two broad aims be considered together. A major reason for attaching high priority to the improvement of the attractiveness of teaching, as a job and as a career, is to enhance its appeal to potential and practising teachers so that good entrants come into teaching and able practitioners do not become disenchanted and leave. Hence, the same policies and measures have the dual ambition of improving the image, conditions, and rewards of teachers and of upholding the competitiveness of teaching in the professional labour market, thereby maintaining or enhancing supply.

Policies with these broad aims in view are largely overlapping, therefore, but they are not identical. Were the purpose of ensuring that teachers are properly rewarded and recognised to arise only through concern over ensuring future supply, those ambitions could be abandoned during periods when, or in those countries where, relative surplus is experienced; that would have evidently retrograde results on motivation, morale, and on the quality of new recruits. Equally, to ensure adequate teacher supply also extends beyond policies explicitly concerned with improving attractiveness. It is closely related to those higher education policies that fix admissions, flows, and the certification of trainee teachers. It is affected by the specially targeted measures, where these exist, aimed at priority groups of teachers such as those in certain shortage subject areas, unattractive geographical regions, and key groups of potential recruits. And, most importantly, supply can only be addressed in relation to the realities of actual, future, and desired demand for teachers. That demand is partially determined by factors largely exogenous to the education system (such as the demographic determinants of student numbers) but also by key policies and choices relating to student retention and participation, the curriculum, and staffing.

The analysis of teacher supply and demand

This chapter will not present a technical analysis of supply of and demand for teachers[18]. That is a well-established branch of study in its own right, often involving highly complicated models incorporating a wide array of variables. The education authorities in many OECD countries employ such models to assist them either in short-run planning or for long-term forecasting though with varying assumptions and differing sets of variables. To report the results even for a single country would require careful documentation and interpretation[19].

The interaction of teacher supply and demand is too complex and open to permit the application of closed forecasting models; indeed, forecasts in this field have proved a notoriously unreliable tool for educational policy-making. The *supply* side is composed of a complex mix of new teachers from higher education, entrants from other backgrounds and returning from a period away from work, practising teachers and their patterns of mobility, quitting, family-raising, or retirement. It involves critical group differences in terms of personal aims and professional alternatives whether between men and women, subject specialists, primary and secondary school teachers in, respectively, the general and vocational fields. It is influenced by a whole array of conditions and factors relating to teachers and teaching including working and social conditions, salaries and other fringe benefits, and more personal, psychological factors, each of which represents a complex cluster of variables. And teacher supply is crucially influenced by all the economic, social, and labour market developments that impinge not only on teaching but on the entire range of occupations and employment sectors that stand in competition for potential and practising teachers.

Demand for teachers is, in some respects, more open-ended still. It is in part determined by the familiar vagaries of demographic change as sketched in Chapter 2, and their corresponding impact on numbers of young people in education and training – highly predictable in the short term, but ill-behaved in relation to the long-term assumptions of forecast models. Far from being a given for planning purposes, demand for teachers itself springs directly from policy decisions, negotiations, and compromises whether concerning such detailed matters as staffing levels and rights to extended leave for in-service teacher training or other purposes, or concerning major reforms in education and training provision. The declared aim in France nearly to double the proportion of youngsters who stay on to receive an education to the level of the *baccalauréat* to attain four-fifths of each cohort by the end of the century, or the establishment of a national curriculum in the traditionally decentralised system of England and Wales under the 1988 Education Act implying the radical expansion of the teaching of certain subjects such as foreign languages, provide but two of the most dramatic illustrations of the policy-determined nature of demand. New vocational programmes outside traditional school settings and the need to provide qualified staff in technical fields subject to very rapid knowledge obsolescence raise their own special demands for teachers, whether new or practising. And the critical choices not only concern the policy-making authorities at national, regional, and local levels; pupils and students themselves exercise a myriad of options in ways that can quickly make a nonsense of the most careful prognoses. The relatively centralised organisation of the French national education system, for example, allows for some of the most elaborate planning among all OECD countries. Official 1986 estimates of total student numbers to be expected in 1996 had, however, already been surpassed at the beginning of the new school year beginning in 1988[20]. In Germany, just as the size of the student cohorts is falling, so are students choosing to fill the existing universities to overflowing.

The conclusions to be drawn extend well beyond the purely technical to embrace considerations of clear policy significance. First, the determinants of teacher supply and demand embrace a complex web of factors beyond those most well-publicised of, on the supply side, salaries and, on the demand side, demographic developments, important though these are. Second, those determinants themselves arise from policy choices and options. They are not simply exogenously given. Indeed, in a sense it is even misleading to talk of the supply of and demand for teachers when education authorities possess substantial powers to intervene on both sides of the equation. Third, *quality* is not to be forgotten in the face of the quantitative calculations. Ensuring supply is about maintaining adequate numbers of *good* teachers, not merely filling vacant posts. Finally, it is important to distinguish between short-term planning and long-term forecasts. The former is a necessary and normal element of all administration. For a long-term perspective, the best that may be achieved is to highlight a number of foreseeable possible or probable developments and their policy implications that together may call for serious attention. If such long-term analyses result in responses that alleviate the foreseen problems, the "predictions" will be proved wrong but their value will be vindicated.

Shortage or surplus? Diverse situations between and within countries

Already in Chapter 1, the emerging perception of new problems concerning teacher supply was underlined as one reason why the condition of teaching has or will become a matter of high public priority. Not all Member countries nor, within them, all regions, schools, and disciplines are or will be equally affected. Nor should concern about future developments be caricatured as the depiction of widespread crisis or the impending collapse of the education service. In the rest of this chapter, aspects of the current situation concerning teacher supply will be discussed, including various pecuniary and non-pecuniary components of the profession's attractiveness. This is concluded by a presentation of possible developments that risk posing serious new problems for this side of education and training policies. Even those countries that today experience relative surpluses may find that situation transformed over the decade ahead.

General descriptions of current national situations concerning teacher shortage and surplus across OECD countries display substantial diversity. At one end of the spectrum are countries like Germany and Ireland, where the phenomenon of teacher unemployment remains the dominant reality. The percentage of probationary teachers hired in Germany on completion of initial training has risen since 1979 from 88 per cent to the quasi-totality (98 per cent) by 1987; the proportion hired on completion of probation reveals instead a dramatically different picture. Having stood at 83.8 per cent at the end of the 1970s, the percentage hired had slumped to only 11.8 per cent by 1986[21]. The Irish report frankly describes the current poor employment prospects of teachers in the following terms:

"Teaching is now difficult to enter, and easy to leave in the sense that a teacher may leave for up to five years while preserving the right to return (career breaks), and emigration has taken a very important place in the range of options available to all Irish people, including teachers.... the employment prospects of trained teachers are excellent, although their prospects of permanent employment as teachers are very poor" (pp. 118 and 121)[22].

Other countries with general surpluses and continuing keen competition for entry to teaching include Belgium[23], and Japan[24].

A number of other OECD countries, however, already report more difficult current staffing and/or recruitment problems, and most refer to particular pockets of teacher shortage. Even in Germany, with such an abundance of candidates, there are recruitment difficulties for teachers in special schools, for religion, music, and the sciences, and for the vocational subjects of food science and study, construction and woodworking, hygiene, clothing, and agriculture. The New Zealand report describes the general difficulty of filling secondary training quotas[25], a problem reported too by France and the United Kingdom. The recent campaign in France to advertise the availability of posts and to stress the positive sides of teaching, and the establishment in England and Wales of a Teacher Shortage Action Programme, including the Teaching as a Career (TASC) unit to promote teacher recruitment, that has conducted a similar, though unprecedentedly national-level campaign[26], indicate that even existing shortages are arousing concern.

The campaigns mentioned above are important in revealing that there is an informational side to the problem as well as the more familiar targets of improving training capacity and/or the attractiveness of the profession. Younger and older potential teachers need to know that openings are available and that special provisions exist that might facilitate their entry into the profession. François Orivel has expressed the "informational" problem vividly by reference to France:

"You can understand the universities and students. Up to 1979-1980, it had become a discouraging experience to sit the competitive entry exams to be a teacher. The number of candidates far outnumbered the few available openings. You needed the level of 'Normale Sup' [higher teacher training college] to get in. And all that only to end up in a provincial CES [comprehensive school]. Everyone was put off. Since 1980, new recruits are being sought once more, but no one knows about that. It's necessary to let them know".[27]

The informational dimension is likely to be even more pertinent for other than highly visible and standardized procedures, such as entry from industry and commerce.

Attention only to aggregate measured surpluses and shortages is, then, to focus on but part of the problem. The importance of the quality of new recruits and of practising teachers has already been emphasized and will be discussed in more detail in the following chapter. But even in more specific ways, shortages can take subtle but very real guises that tend to remain hidden from public view. One country has adopted a three-way classification to describe these[28]:

a) *Overt shortages.* This is the classic, most obvious form of shortage, in which there are vacancies for particular types of teacher which cannot be filled.

b) *Hidden shortage.* In this case, teaching is given in a subject by a teacher inadequately qualified in the subject.

c) *Suppressed shortage.* In this case, overt or hidden shortages are concealed by giving inadequate provision for certain subjects in the timetable.

The latter category in particular is likely to defy measurement. It represents the hidden but potentially dramatic case where a school's provision or a country's policies are diverted altogether and potentially jeopardized through lack of adequately trained staff. It may refer to foreign languages, to the introduction of information technologies into the classroom, to chemistry, or to music. Clear, comprehensive information at the national level on these different dimensions of staffing shortage, especially where overt and hidden, would shed significant light on the contemporary conditions of teaching. Understanding the situation concerning "suppressed" shortages – where existing trained teacher stock simply does not match official ambitions – will in all likelihood require analyses of a different order than head-counting.

It has been emphasized that the regional and disciplinary dimensions of teacher surplus and shortage are critical. Teacher shortages in certain regions or subjects may, of course, represent no more than the "frictional" lag of trained teachers adjusting to new conditions or programmes, though in the interim students will have been affected. Or, such shortages may prove to be more deep-rooted and patterned. If they turn out to be widespread and chronic, whether geographical or more especially in particular subjects such as in the sciences or technical fields, then they cannot be minimised as merely sectoral. They are then, *de facto*, general shortages.

Analyses conducted in the United States in the mid-1980s are revealing (though the passage of even 3 to 4 years makes them already dated). One prominent commentator expressed scepticism concerning exaggerated reports of a teacher shortage crisis across the nation as a whole[29] though federal estimates were less sanguine. Wagner underlined the importance of the distributional, rather than the aggregate, aspects of supply and demand:

"The larger problem may well be maldistribution – both geographically and across specialities – of the available supply. With respect to the former, rates of growth in school enrollments are projected to vary widely by city, state, and region. Schools in most major cities are expected to experience enrollment increases substantially higher than the five per cent estimated for the nation as a whole. Enrollments in sun belt states and California, fuelled principally by relatively large increases in minority enrollments, are also expected to increase more rapidly. In these areas, the pool of those qualified and willing to teach at current pay levels and conditions may well fall short of the demand for additional teachers. Evidence of shortages also appears in several fields" (p. 10)[30].

Similar examples could be elaborated for all OECD countries. Depressed city centres, isolated rural districts, expensive housing areas, are commonly the regions that face severe problems of recruitment. For subjects, difficulties arise especially where the output of higher education graduates in specific fields has slumped through lack of employment outlets, or where the competition from other employment sectors is intense and difficult to counter (such as it is for specialists in the physical sciences, business, and a variety of technological subjects) or where the speed of change of knowledge and technical processes renders the lack of up-to-date staff a permanent problem and challenge.

The array of policy measures in place to combat these two sources of teacher shortage is already extensive. In part, these aim to improve overall attractiveness of the profession (discussed below). But they embrace too a variety of targeted financial measures. These include additional bursaries or grants for teachers who train in priority subjects[31], inexpensive loans, or displacement and removal allowances[32], and special bonuses for those willing to teach in unpopular regions. For the latter, the Norwegian report indicates that even with specific inducements, the problem of attracting well-qualified staff to the north of the country is still not overcome:

"The distribution of unqualified teachers in the country is very uneven. In southern Norway, the percentage was, with few exceptions, less than 4 per cent in 1986. In the three northern counties it was as high as about 11 per cent, in the northernmost as high as 16 per cent..... Teachers in many districts in the northernmost parts of the country have somewhat higher salaries and other economic advantages (cheap housing, sabbatical leaves, study-loans paid by the state)... these are arrangements to stimulate recruitment of qualified teachers in this region" (pp. 2 and 15)[33].

The problems are such, in other words, that differentiated pay is required.

The Swedish report refers to the government commitment to go even one step further. The intention is to pay "market salary additions" to boost recruitment in selected technical and vocational fields[34]. The proposition that certain teachers should be paid more than others because they face particular competition from other industrial and commercial fields often encounters general opposition from teacher representatives similar to their reaction to the notion of "merit pay". How far such bonuses may become viewed as a necessity will depend in part on how severe are the shortages that inflict the different disciplines. One practical difficulty with implementing such schemes of "shortage premiums" may be that cyclical changes may constantly alter the fields where these are acute. It may also be that many, and a growing proportion of, technical and vocational teachers would need to receive the additional money for the schemes to be effective in terms of inducing higher recruitment and retention. The *level* at which these bonuses would need to be fixed to influence career decisions may also prove to be prohibitively high. Cuthbert's study of teachers in the scientific and other fields[35] raises a further delicate consideration if the intention were to make additional payments for science teachers in secondary schools: it would result in the anomalous situation of paying the graduates with the poorer results (in Scotland as probably elsewhere, science teachers have a higher proportion of third-class and pass degrees) more money.

The attractiveness of teaching

Salaries

That many of the specific measures cited above depend on financial inducements and incentives serves to underline that the level of financial rewards constitutes an essential aspect, if only one, of the overall attractiveness of any occupation. This applies more than ever in today's costly societies typified by growth in social aspirations and in consumer expectations. In both the distant and recent past across OECD countries, teachers' salaries have been sensitive to the economic forces of relative shortage and surplus: the 1960s in many OECD countries witnessed rising relative rewards for teachers that then, it would seem, tended to slip back, especially compared with certain occupational groups particularly in commerce, business, and skilled manual trades. The slippage was also an aspect of the general constraint under which the public sector was held and relates to the differing rewards available in the public and private domains[36].

While salary levels, let us reiterate, are but one of the entire package of costs and benefits related to an occupation in determining its attractiveness, it cannot be denied that they are an especially important feature of it. Cross-country analysis in the field is, however, far from straightforward. Comparisons present a minefield of methodological as well as political problems. The array of financial benefits, non-pecuniary conditions, working hours and days that characterise teachers' rewards vary so widely that simple comparisons of pay levels – that are well-known and publicly available in each individual country – are as likely to fuel invidious comparisons as they are to provide illumination concerning teachers' living standards and just deserts. One of the most careful international studies concluded thus:

"The primary conclusion from this examination of average teacher salaries concerns data acquisition and data quality rather than substance. Piecing together a multicountry data base from diverse individual country sources seems not to be a good strategy for making serious international comparisons. There are simply too many unanswered questions about the data for one to have much confidence in the results. Such work requires a more thorough and systematic approach – one that yields well-documented salary data plus enough contextual information to support interpretations of intercountry comparisons" (pp. 30-31)[37].

Still more are the methodological complexities magnified when the purpose is to demonstrate trends through time rather than present a snapshot picture.

It is, nevertheless, instructive to examine detailed aspects of teachers' financial rewards. A basic variable is the progression of salary levels over the career. Countries differ in both the period of time it takes to reach the top of the incremental career ladder and the gap between starting salaries and maximum levels. Data published in the joint Dutch/European Commission study in 1988, reorganised and reproduced in Table 7, illustrate the scale of these variations (the relevant point here being the variations; actual magnitudes and ratios may well since have altered in the course of recent pay negotiations).

The table shows, in addition, that there is no necessary relation between salary trajectories, in terms of the differences between the top and the bottom, and the age at which the former is reached. For instance, England and Wales display a relatively wide gap between the lowest and top salary levels, yet the maximum can be reached at a comparatively young age. The opposite is true in Italy. The scale of these differences shows that room exists for the exercise of policy choice, not only in terms of the levels of teachers' salaries, but also in how they are structured and evolve over the career. In weighing alternative structures, relevant considerations include the relative priority attached to attracting young recruits or to retaining good teachers and providing the incentive of a long career ladder. How beneficial is it, for instance, for the able teacher to be rapidly rewarded with tangible pay increases if the maximum is soon attained and the only alternative for improvement is promotion out of the classroom?

Looking beyond Europe, comparisons of the salaries of Japanese and United States teachers have accorded significance to the steeper and more protracted career structure in Japan[38]. Analysis of the recent improvements that have been witnessed in the average annual salary of public school teachers in the United States – $22 664 in 1980/81, rising to $23 955 in 1983/84 and $26 551 in 1986/87 in constant dollars[39] – have also suggested that it is the young teachers who have benefited more than their experienced colleagues[40].

Table 7
TEACHERS' SALARIES[a] IN PRIMARY AND SECONDARY EDUCATION IN SELECTED EEC COUNTRIES: RATIOS[b] OF MINIMUM TO MAXIMUM LEVELS AND POSSIBLE AGE FOR ATTAINING THE MAXIMUM

Country	Primary		Secondary	
	Index max/min	Maximum at age	Index max/min	Maximum at age
Belgium	1.68	49	* 1.80 ** 1.84	49
Denmark	1.33	41	* 1.33 ** 1.50	41
England and Wales	2.03	35	2.46	39
France	1.54	45	* 1.65 ** 1.93	48 46.5
Germany	1.48	33	* 1.46 ** 1.57	46 48
Netherlands	2.01	46	* 1.98 ** 2.14	44 45
Ireland	1.89	45	1.89	45
Italy	1.43	58	* 1.46 ** 1.48	63
Luxembourg	2.34	45	* 1.78 ** 1.78	46 48
Scotland	1.56	33	1.53	32

a) In national currencies: for methods of calculations, see source.
b) Defined as the maximum salary divided by the minimum salary for each salary scale.

General note: This table reproduces without revision the figures contained in the original source. It is necessary to consult the country data on which this report is based for the precise criteria for inclusion (for example, salaries in the Great Britain examples include teachers but exclude heads and deputy heads) and for the methods of calculating the "maximum age"; these are not OECD figures.

Country notes: */**
Belgium: Regent/licentiaat; *Denmark:* Laerer/magister; *France:* PEGC/professeurs certifiés; *Germany:* Realschullehrer/gymnasial Lehrer; *Netherlands:* Leraar 2/leraar 1; *Italy:* Docente scala 7/docente scala 7 bis; *Luxembourg:* Professeur d'enseignement technique/professeur.
Source: ECSC-EEC-EAEC (1988), *The Conditions of Service of Teachers in the European Community,* Brussels and Luxembourg, Appendix I, Tables 1a) and 2a). (Based on national data from 2-3 years before date of publication).

A further detailed aspect of teachers' salaries that deserves attention is their differential attractiveness for women compared with men.

Published data are scattered but Swedish[41] and Australian[42] figures are indicative. In the Swedish case, for example, whereas the monthly salary of a female junior-level teacher in 1985 ranked fifth in the classification adopted (improving from eighth in 1980), for a man the equivalent ranking was twelfth (though improving from fourteenth at the earlier date). Australian comparisons of teacher pay with other graduate salaries show that for men, despite all the male advantages of seniority, their averages were well below those for comparably aged male graduates and a salary structure that is "particularly flat compared to that in other occupations for graduates". In fact, such a finding indicates more about the labour market rewards and opportunities available for women than it does about teachers' pay *per se*. The well-documented overall earnings differentials by sex automatically means that, at the same rates of pay, teaching is better rewarded for women, *relative to other female workers*, than it is for men, compared with other males. Combined with certain other advantages of teaching, such as the convenience of time schedules for parents with school-age children, the feminisation of teaching derives a certain rationale. Yet lest that should be regarded as grounds for assuming that an abundant source of teacher supply – women teachers – is well assured, the indications are, on the contrary, that this comparative advantage is being eroded. In fact, it is one of the main factors highlighted below for concern about the future.

Discussion of financial rewards raises too the controversial issue of pecuniary supplements for "merit" and as additional incentives. Attitudes, within and across countries, differ sharply on this matter. In some, both teachers and the authorities regard the notion of the "master" or, in more gender-neutral terms, "expert" or "lead" teacher, as alien. In others, the notion of expertise is recognised by special status but not with additional financial reward[43]. In yet others, the notion of providing financial incentives is either under serious discussion or else initiatives have been undertaken and are already in place. This matter lay at the heart of recent debates in France. In the United Kingdom, the new pay structure introduced in 1987 included for the first time a system of incentive allowances intended to be received partly by those adjudged to be of outstanding merit though that component of the incentive award has, at the time of writing, not been implemented[44]. The designation of "lead" teachers is one feature of the through-going reorganisation of the education system currently being implemented in New Zealand[45]. And there are many experiments with merit pay schemes (and the related concept of "career ladders") in the United States, with an accompanying, rapidly burgeoning literature[46]. Needless to say, that literature covers a wide spread of views concerning the value and effectiveness of such supplements.

A number of general observations can be made about these particular measures and proposals. First, sensitivity to language and terminology should not be neglected in this domain; whether the incentive is provided solely through an addition to the cheque or whether there is a new title and what that is – "expert", "master", "lead" – matters. Second, whether incentive allowances are viewed as an *additional* spur to effort or instead as an *alternative* to across-the-board payments will greatly affect their acceptability and likely success. Third, such incentives will probably be much more visible to practising teachers than to those outside the profession. If enacted, their probable target will more nearly be the goals of enhancing quality or raising motivation than of attracting new recruits. The scale and relative availability of such awards are also likely to influence their reception. If they are minor financial extras or rarely awarded, their effect is also likely to be minimal. In the United Kingdom example referred toearlier, there is provision for some 55 per cent of teachers to receive incentive allowances by autumn 1989 (though this covers a wider set of cases than reward for "outstanding" teaching)[47].

To conclude, if they are to act as incentives, "merit pay" systems must be largely acceptable to those for whom they are intended – namely, the teachers themselves. If outright opposition persists once such schemes are in place, their target is likely to be missed. Yet it can also be observed that the actual principle of differentiated pay is already an accepted, even entrenched, feature of teachers' salary structures. Issues of fairness and of how "merit" is assessed are clearly no less important than the issue of whether a further tier of differentiation should be introduced into existing salary scales. As the array of schemes and proposals involving financial supplements for different purposes grows, so does the value of undertaking detailed analyses and evaluations of their different features and effects.

Non-financial rewards and conditions

Each country has its own wealth of surveys and data on teachers that shed light on the different aspects of their work they find frustrating or rewarding, disenchanting or stimulating. The different facets of non-pecuniary rewards and conditions may be revealed by the relatively "hard" evidence of institutional arrangements and such indicators as teacher absence due to illness (increasing in many OECD countries) or wastage rates (still generally lower than alarmist journalistic reports tend to warn of) though both of these indicators reflect a wider range of factors than those strictly related to schools and classrooms. Or they may rely on the "soft" data of questionnaires and in-depth observation to get behind the administrative facts and raw figures. All these factors, the pecuniary and the non-precuniary, the objective and the subjective, are interactive. To isolate one factor – whether salaries, fringe benefits, class size, or school routines and working hours – is likely to be misleading without due attention to the realities and perceptions of teaching taken as a whole. One fact that is noteworthy, however, is the significance that teachers attach to the various non-pecuniary rewards and difficulties of their job. Fogarty expressed it thus:

> "Conventional wisdom says that adequate salaries, more in line with those of persons with comparable education, are the answer... Certainly this writer's frequent conversations with teachers bring to the question 'What would make teaching a better life for you?' the same response: 'A decent salary!' However, when the conversation is taken a step further, to the question 'With a better salary, would you be happy in teaching?' the response is often a hesitation, followed by 'No, because.. ' leading to a discussion of the many factors that make teaching so grindingly debilitating"[48].

Many of the national reports underline the frequency with which teachers refer to such concerns as "powerlessness", and "inability to see the job through to a satisfactory conclusion" as among the most problematic aspects of their work.

A number of general features of the nature of teachers' work can be emphasized in this section which, while not equally applicable to all schools, colleges, communities, and countries, help delineate with more clarity the professional and social conditions of teaching. First, there is the relative isolation in which most teachers work. The single teacher in front of a classroom of youngsters and solely responsible for their learning is the norm across OECD countries. Attempts to reduce that isolation will often meet with fierce resistance, not least from teachers themselves who may well see such efforts as an erosion of their professional autonomy. But the personal cost is a heavy one. Very few other jobs place such binding faith in the organisational unit of the solitary professional.

A second particularity of teachers' work is the small degree to which the nature of the job changes from the beginning of the career through to the end at departure from the classroom. This lack of differentiation is a serious disincentive to professional development and to remaining in teaching itself, even when that would be the teacher's first choice. The different concepts of "lead" teacher, as referred to above, should thus make the questions of professional and career development central. We return to the question of improving the attractiveness of careers in teaching at the end of this chapter.

A further feature of the work of teachers is how physically and mentally fatiguing the task of teaching actually is. That fatigue is magnified further if the teacher is confronting difficult students or managing with poor facilities. Teaching involves hundreds, even thousands, of interactions daily. The reality of teacher fatigue is a qualification to the sweeping conclusions sometimes drawn from the effective schooling research literature advocating the maximisation of "time on task"; this should be seen as the advocacy of the effective use of classroom time for learning rather than the assumption either that the balance of teaching to working but non-teaching time should be ever tipped in favour of the former or that the individual's capacity for extra teaching is limitless. Fatigue and the need for renewal should help inform decisions about leave of absence and in-service training. But it should also be borne in mind that not all teacher time is devoted to classroom teaching, whether in the working day or in the calendar year. In those countries in particular that are characterised by comparatively short academic years, long vacations (especially in the summer), and where teaching is the main job held, the argument that some additional preparation or training should be conducted during non-teaching time can only be partially countered by reference to the stresses and fatigue peculiar to the job of teaching. There is room for exploration, in these cases, of the extension of professional, non-teaching duties when the students are still on vacation outside the normal school year.

Finally, teachers in general face unenviable pressures that derive from the fact that all of the country's population have, at one time or another, attended school. Many people in the population at large, particularly recent generations, have undertaken extensive educational careers incorporating advanced studies. This contributes significantly to the relatively intangible but nonetheless real social reactions that fuel the feeling of malaise and loss of recognition that so many teachers complain of. For one thing, it can breed significant underlying resentment towards teachers – from pupils and students who are given no choice about attendance at school, from parents and the adult population in general harbouring long-standing ill feeling. Such collective sentiments, and the implications they hold for teachers, have figured relatively little in the sociology of education to date. Universal education also means that all can lay claim to educational "expertise" based on their own experiences, no matter how partial the judgement or dated that experience. This is reinforced by the essentially subjective nature of educational results – knowledge, skills, values, habits, and attitudes. Invaluable though parental involvement and a broad base of participation in educational decision-making undoubtedly are, they nevertheless leave the teacher at the middle of a unique tension between professional isolation and public exposure.

FUTURE DEVELOPMENTS

Internal and external forces constraining teacher supply

Looking out on the future is necessarily an uncertain exercise but a number of developments are already in train that may well exercise a profound influence on education, and on the issues of recruitment and supply in particular, in years to come. Whether they add up to a prognosis of "crisis" is only to be assessed in the specific terms of each national situation. Four global developments are presented below, two of them, so to speak, "internal" to education and training systems, two deriving from the broader economic and social context in which they are placed.

The first concerns a major "internal" factor which has already been examined in Chapter 2 – the ageing of the teaching forces of OECD countries. The general conclusion drawn there was that they were "ageing but not yet aged". The complementary conclusion was, though, that the effects of the "greying" of the profession are becoming ever more apparent (one national report to the OECD enquiry presents a detailed analysis of foreseen retirement patterns and its wide implications for recruitment needs)[49]. That the "bulge" of

61

teacher numbers corresponding to the major recruitment drives of the 1960s and early 1970s is not on the immediate verge of retirement does provide some leeway in which to implement coherent strategies to boost recruitment. Yet by the very nature of the problem, with the passage of time, that leeway diminishes and ultimately disappears.

The second "internal" development concerns the complex, unpredictable interplay between demographic trends and educational demand as they affect both the number of pupils, students, and trainees to be taught, on one side, and the number of students coming through the higher education systems of OECD countries to enter the potential pool of new teachers, on the other. Modest reversals of the long-term decline in births that some countries are now experiencing (see Table 2) have an inevitable if lagged effect of producing a growth of pupil numbers in primary schools, while lower secondary school rolls continue to fall in many countries. Meanwhile, still increasing rates of female participation in the labour force, among other things, have exercised a powerful influence on the demand for pre-primary provision, while the rapidly burgeoning post-compulsory sector will continue to call for substantial numbers of new staff. Coincident with these diverse and changing demands, the impact of demographic and enrolment trends affect student numbers in the higher education systems that constitute a major source of new teacher supply. The United Kingdom report presents this coincidence of factors to note that, in that country at least, they operate in clear contradiction to one another:

> "The falling birth rate in the United Kingdom in the 1970s translates itself into a fall in secondary pupil numbers in the 1980s and a consequent fall in the numbers of qualified young people between the ages of 18 to 26 in the middle to late 1990s. It is from such a pool that most teachers are normally recruited. At the same time a recovery in the birth rate in the 1980s translates itself into rising primary pupil numbers from 1986 onwards, causing the total pupil number figure to rise again, albeit gradually, from 1991 onwards. This suggests a rising demand for teachers from 1991 just when the cohort of people from whom new teachers are overwhelmingly drawn shrinks to its smallest"[50].

Were future supply and demand questions to be decided purely by factors internal to education and training systems, the challenge posed to recruitment policies would already be imposing. But attention to the changing "external" labour market environment suggests a different source of difficulty. The paragraph from which the above quotation is drawn is completed with the sentence: "competition from other sectors of the economy for such manpower, particularly for graduates in technical subjects, is likely to be intense". That could well prove to be one of the causes for gravest concern for the maintenance of future teacher supply. With economic recovery and a smaller graduate cohort coming into the labour market, the well-rehearsed contemporary difficulties of attracting good recruits to teaching in the face of the competition from industry and commerce offering greater rewards may well become still worse. In other words, measures to improve the attractiveness of the teaching profession, if they succeed, may only be sufficient to prevent it from slipping still further behind.

Whether the scale of change will result in general skill shortages or whether sharpened competition will be felt mainly in certain sectors of the labour market typified by rapid change and high skill requirements remains a matter of contention. Whichever way it is resolved, the *OECD Employment Outlook* projections, comparing present with future labour market and population numbers, lend support to the general thesis of greater competition of education and training systems as employers with other employment sectors for new recruits. For, taking all the countries for which data are available[51], the smallest 10-year cohort between ages 15 and 45 foreseen in the year 2000 is that aged 15-25. In all cases, the size of this cohort is foreseen to be smaller than it was in 1987. And in all cases again, the numbers within this cohort expected to be in the labour force will fall. Competition will thus probably intensify. The likely effects of this is a matter of concern not only to education but equally to other areas of public employment that have traditionally relied on major inflows of young adults and these include the military services and the health sector. The competition is thus not only with industry and commerce; it is also with other service sectors confronting similar recruitment difficulties.

The fourth major factor covered in this section may also be seen as an "external" influence on the dynamics of education systems, namely, the labour market behaviour and experiences of women. Not only do female teachers represent a major proportion of the teaching force at any one time (see the previous chapter) but they constitute a vital source of supply through the numbers who return to teaching after a period away for family or other reasons. Women should thus constitute a key focus of policies designed to combat possible shortages, especially in those countries where diminishing enrolment in the higher education segment of the potential pool of teachers increases the importance of its other segments (returners, non-traditional entrants, etc.).

The vital role of women as a source of teacher supply is beyond question. What remains to be established is why that role should be a reason for concern in the years ahead. In fact, there is more than one worrying aspect here. (It is to be emphasized that this relates specifically to the question of educational and teaching policies; from the viewpoint of the social and economic position of women in general the same developments may be viewed quite differently).

Changes already in evidence suggest caution concerning the abundance of the supply of women teachers. For, as women's labour market attitudes and experience are coming more nearly to resemble those of men, especially for the college-educated, then the same factors that discourage males from entering and staying in teaching come to apply similarly to females. Such convergence is apparent from a number of indicators. Overall female labour force participation rates are still increasing (Table 5), life-cycle participation patterns show a greater propensity to continuous employment or to shorter breaks from work than in the past, women's presence in a variety of prestigious occupational fields such as law and medicine has grown, even dramatically in some OECD countries, and female college students' attitudes towards work and careers show convergence with those of men[52]. If the labour market situation of the 1990s does develop into one of shortages in high-skill sectors and of keener competition for recruits, as is likely, the growing work and career ambitions of women may only be expected to continue apace. Teaching may not fare well in the choices then made by talented, well-educated women, unless, of course, it changes to become a more attractive prospect to them.

Two additional considerations may also prove to be significant here. First, most countries report that the recruitment of new teachers has, over the past decade, increasingly shifted from young trainees to more experienced "returners" and entrants from other fields. To some extent, therefore, there is already heavy reliance on the women who belong to this section of the potential pool. They should not be regarded as an infinite resource. Second, those programmes and disciplines that already tend to suffer from the most severe shortages and/or have become high priorities for expansion – especially such subjects as physics, chemistry, technology and design, the technical and vocational fields – are precisely those with fewest women teachers. Unless general policies will effect a major shift in female choices in school and college education[53], it cannot be assumed that women will provide for the shortfalls in these subjects, if and as they occur.

63

Key policy implications

How these developments will apply across OECD countries in the decade ahead remains to be seen. They cannot be assumed to add up to the certain collapse of teacher supply – adjustments of behaviour and policy have in the past proved the direst warnings to be exaggerated and the future simply holds too many unknowns. Nor will the consequences of these developments, where they do occur, all be negative. With the retirement of growing numbers of older teachers, for example, so will promotional opportunities be opened up for their younger colleagues that would have remained blocked in the past. The above developments and scenarios do, nevertheless, amount to a set of powerful reasons for directing very serious attention to policies for teachers and for improving the attractiveness of the profession.

Concerning *teacher training*, a demanding conclusion that derives from the above is that both pre-service and in-service training will be, if anything, of even higher priority than hitherto. The capacity and quality of *pre-service* education are vital for meeting existing and future shortages. Yet that capacity has suffered drastic cutbacks in many OECD countries over the recent past, while quality, as discussed in the next chapter, remains an area where improvements can undoubtedly still be realised. The challenges here are thus imposing. It will certainly be important to resist the temptation, if teacher shortages become more severe, of believing that the relaxation of training standards is an option in the hope that greater numbers can thereby be recruited. The aim, to repeat, is to ensure an adequate supply of high-quality teachers.

The arguments for more extensive *in-service* education and training of teachers (INSET) are more compelling than ever. With very large numbers of practising teachers destined to remain in the profession for the next 10, 15, 20 years or more, the dual ambitions of enhancing the responsiveness of education in the face of change and of improving the professional standing and satisfaction of teachers both point to the key role of INSET. The resource implications of continued or still greater priority to be accorded to both pre-service and in-service teacher training at the same time may prove daunting, especially in the light of the costs of other aspects of teacher policies. For this reason alone, the potential of school-based in-service teacher education should be fully exploited.

The aims of enhancing the responsiveness of the profession to change and familiarity with other employment settings, teacher quality, as well as meeting existing and possibly worsening shortages, all point towards *encouraging entrants to teaching from other occupational backgrounds*. Those aims suggest giving serious attention to preparation and qualifications in higher education – whether mainly for teaching or for other fields – that equip the student with the "polyvalence" to permit greater mobility both into and out of teaching. The search for new sources of teaching staff should be continued and promoted. Yet so long as the profession suffers from problematic recognition and appeal, as it does in many countries, it should not be supposed that tapping those sources will be straightforward, nor will it necessarily result in the hiring of full-time, full-year teachers. Part-time, job-sharing arrangements may often be more appropriate. Potential pitfalls should also be signalled. "Polyvalent" pre-service qualifications should not mean the unacceptable dilution of actual preparation for teaching, nor can teachers entering through non-traditional routes be expected to withstand the rigours of classroom life without receiving proper preparation and follow-up support. Job-sharing and mobility schemes, especially in those technical and vocational fields with ample opportunities for employment elsewhere, may actually result in a net flow out of, not into, the teaching force. Perversely, the result of good contacts with other sectors of employment, of mobility and job-sharing measures, and of appropriate in-

64

service training programmes to keep staff up-to-date can actually be that the education system acts as an employment agency for other enterprises. Schools and colleges may thus become "victims of their own success".

Policies aimed primarily at meeting shortfalls in certain key subjects through the establishment of non-traditional routes for workers and professionals with diverse backgrounds and experiences may also be justified in terms of improving the quality of the teaching force. Whether or not they do have that effect in practice can, however, only be decided on the basis of established criteria and concrete evidence. Diversity of background alone is no guarantee of the qualities that provide for the effective communication of knowledge and skills to students. On the other hand, it is likely that the maturity, experience of different life settings, and the professional motivation implied in realising a significant career change predispose non-traditional entrants, if carefully chosen, to become good teachers. Once selected, the key requirements for such entrants are then, at the least, a useful and well-tailored introduction to education and teaching and guaranteed recourse to professional support.

Finally, the aim of improving *careers in teaching* requires special consideration. Maintaining teacher supply is obviously as much about retaining good teachers as it is of attracting new staff. In part, this means attention to such variables as salary scales and the possibilities for and timing of progression through different promotional posts as discussed earlier in this chapter.

Yet the options for improving the attractiveness of teaching as a career can extend beyond altering the administrative framework within which teachers are paid and promoted. It implies, for instance, redressing the marked imbalances between the sexes in leadership positions. If women are to continue to constitute an important source of future teacher supply, that will call for their calculus of its attractiveness as a career, not just as a job, to be positive. That implies paying close attention to selection criteria and procedures for promotion. If imbalances change little despite that attention, the case for quotas should be considered. Either way, it will be necessary to scrutinise carefully the general received ideas and stereotypes about male and female teachers. The more demanding step is to ensure that such generalisations, even when they receive some support in the aggregate, do not enter the judgements of individual cases. For instance, many female teachers are not married, or are not mothers, or are not mothers of young children (though this is not to presume that these factors in any way preclude promotion) despite the tendency to describe the situation of all women in teaching as if these conditions obtain. Selection and promotion, in other words, must apply rigorous and objective procedures.

Improving career structures may also mean questioning the predominant practice of teachers continuing full-time, full-year right up to a fixed retirement age. For experienced teachers, more flexible combinations of classroom teaching with other roles and duties within the school, as well as possible part-time arrangements with educational administrations or other enterprises, may prove to be administratively complex but to yield beneficial results. They may significantly reduce teacher fatigue and burnout while enabling some who so wish to continue work beyond the current retirement age. They may also open up differentiated tasks and opportunities "downwards" so acting as incentives to younger teachers. They may allow for special positions of "lead" teacher to be created without carrying implications of being "first among equals". In sum, they may prove a valuable way to enhance the overall attractiveness of teaching as a career. Here too is a field where further information and, where possible, evaluation on a cross-national basis could prove highly valuable, bearing in mind that, as with many of the best educational ideas, the locus of innovation will often be at the local level.

NOTES AND REFERENCES

1. Etzioni, A. (1969), *The Semi-Professions and their Organisation: Teachers, Nurses, and Social Workers*, New York.

2. Perkin, H. (1983), "The Teaching Profession and the Game of Life", in Gordon, P. (ed.), *Is Teaching a Profession?*, University of London, Institute of Education.

3. OECD (1979), *Teacher Policies in a New Context*, Paris, p. 20.

4. Darling-Hammond, L., Wise, A.E., and Pease, S.R. (1983), "Teacher Evaluation in the Organisational Context: A Review of the Literature", *Review of Educational Research*, Vol. 53, No. 3, pp. 285-328.

5. As discussed in Lawton, D. (1986), "The Role and Professional Status of the Teacher: Some Sociological Perspectives" (OECD working document).

6. The latter developments are discussed in detail in a recent OECD study of the organisation and content of studies in education and training at the post-compulsory phase; OECD (1989), *Pathways for Learning: Education and Training from 16 to 19*, Paris.

7. Neave, G. (1987), "Challenges Met: Trends in Teacher Education 1975-1985", Introduction to *New Challenges for Teachers and their Education: National Reports on Teacher Education*, Council of Europe, Strasbourg.

8. Hostmark-Tarrou, A.-L. (1988), "La formation des professeurs d'enseignement secondaire en Norvège: l'expérience des deux dernières années" (OECD working document, French text only), p. 11.

9. Presentation at a meeting of the Council of Europe on the *Recruitment and Training of Teachers in Vocational and Technical Education*, held in Strasbourg, 7-8 December 1988.

10. See the analysis and issues presented in OECD (1989), *Education and the Economy in a Changing Society*, Paris.

11. Dorrego, B.G. (1988), "Les enseignants en Espagne" (OECD working document, French text only), p. 25.

12. Da Cunha, P. (1989), "Teachers in Portugal" (OECD working document), p. 10.

13. Neave, G. (1987), *op. cit.*, p. 5.

14. Trow, M. (1974), "Problems in the Transition from Elite to Mass Higher Education", in *Policies for Higher Education*, OECD, Paris.

15. The latest evidence for OECD countries as a whole is to be found in OECD (1988), *OECD Employment Outlook*, Chapter 5, "Women's Activity, Employment, and Earnings: A Review of Recent Developments", Paris.

16. One international source covering a number of countries and occupations/industries is found in OECD (1988), "Equal Pay/Comparable Worth", Australian national report to the Working Party on the Role of Women in the Economy.

17. Hodge, R.W. *et al.* (1966), "A Comparative Study of Occupational Prestige in the United States", in Bendix, R. and Lipset, S.M. (eds.) *Class, Status, and Power: Social Comparative Perspective*, Free Press, New York, quoted in Hoyle, E. (1985), "Teachers' Social Backgrounds"

in Husén, T. and Postlethwaite, T.N. (eds.) *The International Encyclopedia of Education* Vol. 9 T-Z, Pergamon Press, Oxford, New York, Toronto, Sydney, Frankfurt.

18. A separate analytical report on teacher supply and demand is under preparation.

19. For one well-documented country study, see Cuthbert, J. (1986), "Assessing Supply and Demand with Particular Reference to Shortage Subjects and Women Teachers – The Case of Scotland" (OECD working document and Statistical Annex).

20. Reported in Petitjean, G. (1989), "Profs: ce qui va changer", *Le Nouvel Observateur*, 19-25 janvier.

21. Jeuthe, E. (1989), "Teachers in Germany: The Employment of Teachers against the Background of Teacher Surplus, the Ageing of the Profession, and a Decline in Student Numbers" (OECD working document).

22. Department of Education (1989), "OECD Review: Ireland. Background Report", Dublin.

23. OECD (1988), "Les enseignants en Belgique néerlandophone" (OECD working document, French text only), p. 8.

24. Maki, M. (1987), "Teachers in Japan" (OECD working document), pp. 2-3.

25. OECD (1988), "Teachers in New Zealand" (OECD working document), p. 24.

26. Discussed in detail in OECD (1988), "Teachers in the United Kingdom: Teacher Supply in England and Wales in an Age of Educational Change" (OECD working document).

27. Quoted in Petitjean, G. (1987), "Profs: La débâcle", *Le Nouvel Observateur,* 4-10 September.

28. Cuthbert, J. (1986), *op. cit.* reporting the classification used by the Department of Education and Science, England and Wales.

29. Feistritzer, C.E. (1986), *Teacher Crisis: Myth or Reality? A State-by-State Analysis*, National Center for Education Information, Washington, D.C.

30. Wagner A. (1987), "Social and Economic Aspects of Teaching: The Attractiveness of the Profession" (OECD working document), drawing on H.L. Hodgkinson (1985), *All One System: Demographics of Education – Kindergarten through Graduate School*, Institute for Educational Leadership. Wagner reports that California, for example, expected to require 85 000 new teachers by 1990. See California Commission on the Teaching Profession (1985), *Who Will Teach Our Children? A Strategy for Improving California's Schools.*

31. See "Teachers in the United Kingdom" *op. cit.*, Appendix A, and Garin, C. (1988), "Comment recruter 300 000 enseignants?", *Le Monde de l'Education*, janvier.

32. For England and Wales, these are described according to a *Times Educational Supplement* survey in "News Focus", 22 July 1988, pp. 8-9.

33. Jordell, K.O. (1989), "Teachers in Norway: With Special Reference to the Supply of and Demand for Teachers in Norway" (OECD working document).

34. Angrén, B., Lovgren, E., and Skog-Ostlin K. (1987), "Teachers in Sweden" (OECD working document), p. 2.

35. Cuthbert, J. (1986), *op. cit.* Section III.

36. Orivel, F. (1987), "Working Conditions and Rewards of Teachers: Methods and Hypotheses" (OECD working document) discusses trends, alert to the innumerable pitfalls that preclude precise quantification. He concludes: "Although available data are often incomplete, it does seem probable that the socio-economic situation of primary and secondary school teachers in the developed countries is deteriorating. Orivel and Perrot, in their study 'Les rémunérations des enseignants dans les pays de l'OCDE, évolution comparative' (IREDU, Dijon, 1985) showed that in most OECD countries the ratio of average teachers' pay to GNP per capita was falling. This would indicate that teachers are not receiving their fair share of the benefits of economic growth, despite the growing tendency of governments to hold on to a mounting percentage of its product. With tighter budgets almost everywhere, any rapid improvement in the teachers' position is unlikely." (p. 26).

37. Barro, S.M. and Suter, L. (1988), "International Comparisons of Teachers' Salaries: An Exploratory Study", Survey Report, National Center for Education Statistics, U.S. Department of Education, Washington D.C. Other references include the now dated source International Labour Organisation (ILO) (1979), *Teachers' Pay*, Geneva, that provides extensive detail on the composition of salaries and pay determination mechanisms but limited quantitative comparisons. More recent European sources include the joint EEC/Netherlands study on the conditions of service of teachers in the European Community carried out by the Stichting Research Group in the Netherlands: ECSC-EEC-EAEC (1988), *The Conditions of Service of Teachers in the European Community*, Brussels, Luxembourg. Extensive material may also be found in World Confederation of Organisations of the Teaching Profession (WCTOP) (1986), *Study on Teachers' Working Conditions in Europe*, Morges, Switzerland, revised edition. For sources that include non-European countries, see Lawton, S.B. (1988), "Teachers' Salaries: An International Perspective", in Alexander, K. and Monk, D.H. *Attracting and Compensating America's Teachers,* Eighth Annual Yearbook of the American Education Finance Association, Bathinger, Cambridge, Mass.; and Barro, S.M. (1986), "A Comparison of Teachers' Salaries in Japan and the United States", report prepared for the NCES, U.S. Department of Education, Washington, D.C.

38. Lawton, S.B. (1988), *ibid.*

39. U.S. Departmemt of Education (1988), *The Digest of Education Statistics: 1988 Edition*, National Center for Education Statistics, Washington, D.C., Table 57.

40. Darling-Hammond, L. and Berry, B. (1988), *The Evolution of Teacher Policy*, Rand/CPRE, Washington D.C.

41. Andrén, B., Lovgren, E. and Skog-Ostlin, K. (1987), *op. cit.*, Table II:12.

42. Burke, G. (1989), "Teachers in Australia: Teacher Supply and Teacher Quality: Social and Economic Aspects" (OECD working document), p. 18. This compares teachers' pay scales with results from the Australian Bureau of Statistics (ABS) 1986 Income Distribution Survey (Cat. No. 6546.0) on the pay of graduates.

43. Oral presentation by the Spanish representative at a meeting of the Working Party on the Condition of Teaching.

44. "Teachers in the United Kingdom" *op. cit.*, Annex G.

45. See Lange, D. (1988), *Tomorrow's Schools: The Reform of Education Administration in New Zealand*, Government printer, Wellington, p. 10.

46. Earlier results are summarised in Wagner, A. (1987), *op. cit.* Another source is Alexander, K. and Monk, D.H. (1988), *op. cit.*, chapters 5-7.

47. "Teachers in the United Kingdom" (1988), *op. cit.*, p. 43.

48. Fogarty, R. (1986), "Teacher Motivations and Attitudes" unpublished paper, School of Education, SUNY, Albany, quoted in Wagner, A. (1987), *op. cit.*, p. 15.

49. "Les enseignants en France" (1988), *op. cit.*, Annex.

50. "Teachers in the United Kingdom" (1988), *op. cit.*, pp. 1-2. Minor revision to the quotation communicated by the relevant national authorities.

51. OECD (1988), *OECD Employment Outlook*, *op. cit.*, Chart 1.3, pp. 42-43. The countries covered are Austria, Canada, Finland, France, Japan, the Netherlands, Norway, Sweden, the United Kingdom, and the United States.

52. A substantial presentation and discussion is to be found in OECD (1988), *OECD Employment Outlook, op. cit.*, Chapter 5.

53. A detailed documentation of the gender distribution of educational opportunities in schools and colleges is to be found in OECD (1986), *Girls and Women in Education*, Paris.

Chapter 4

THE TEACHING PROCESS: RESEARCH AND POLICY

INTRODUCTION

The focus now changes. Having examined to now the broader questions concerning the political setting within which teacher policies are developed, the composition of personnel, and the key matters of status and supply, attention turns more closely on to the teaching process itself. The broad focus of the preceding chapters, essential though it is to policy development in these fields, risks losing from view the ultimate aim of ensuring a high quality education in classrooms, schools, and colleges unless complemented by a closer educational understanding. In this chapter, we consider the activity of teaching itself, through selected research findings and through policies, generalising beyond specific educational settings or the new curricular demands that the modern teacher is confronted with. Those new concrete tasks and challenges are then examined in the next chapter.

The strengths and limitations of the international perspective have already become apparent in the foregoing chapters. When the subject is the complex, unique teaching/learning process that takes place in individual classrooms or workshops, the danger of overly sweeping generalisation becomes a very real one. The coverage of this chapter is thus deliberately and highly selective. The research review presented in the next section refers only to findings generated in the United States. And American research itself represents a vast and constantly growing corpus of knowledge and the present review, based on a commissioned OECD study by Marshall Smith and Jennifer O'Day[1], makes no pretence to comprehensiveness. The United States research tradition, rather than that of another country, has been summarised here for a simple, compelling reason: the substantial weight of educational investigation has come from there. And the review itself belongs in this report because the lessons of enquiry should substantially inform policy debate, even if they provide few unequivocal guidelines. The value of research is more to stimulate new insight and perspectives, and to expose partial or false hypotheses, than it is to suggest ready-made answers. And even for the single North American tradition discussed here, it needs to be recognised that the research points in differing, sometimes conflicting, directions.

The discussion of policies, which comprises the latter part of this chapter, is also highly selective (a complementary CERI project on teacher education and training gives a much more substantial treatment of developments and issues in that field). Ultimately, all educational policies have some impact, directly or indirectly, on classroom practice and so arguably are all relevant here. But two policy domains – teacher education and teacher assessment – have been singled out as being of particular pertinence to the aim of improving teaching, especially as each has attracted considerable debate over recent years with new policy initiatives. For each, the treatment in this chapter is the same: to elaborate certain of

69

the key implications arising from the research review and then to examine concrete policy developments and proposals across a range of OECD countries, beyond simply the United States.

THE RESEARCH REVIEW

The substantial development of research

For centuries few questioned that teachers and teaching were significant elements in the educational process. With increased emphasis on large-scale quantitative research in the 1960s, however, reports began to appear with titles such as "Do Teachers Make a Difference?" or, defensively, "Teachers Make a Difference" [2]. At root, the sceptics did not challenge the importance of the overall effects of teachers and teaching – in other words, one could scarcely conduct education *without* teachers. Their questions focused instead on differential effects: Are teachers with certain experiences and characteristics more effective than other teachers? Are there certain ways or methods of teaching that are more productive than others? Despite the researchers' nuances, however, the inconclusiveness left the impression in the public eye that the importance in general of schooling and teachers had been overestimated.

Over the past 25 years, the research literature addressing these and similar questions has grown very considerably. Where there were once two or three studies on a topic, there are now syntheses ("meta-analyses") of scores and hundreds of them. That there has been greater activity, however, does not guarantee that there are agreed answers to the questions. Indeed, it may well be that this abundance of research has generated more questions than it has answered.

Assumptions and methodologies differ widely. To some, the important questions can be answered by focusing on interactions within the classroom; to others, these cannot be interpreted without examining the context in which the classroom is located, the climate of the school, the nature of the students' home experiences, and so forth; to still others, classroom interactions can only be understood through the subject matter being taught. Concerning methodologies, the largest schism is between those who typically address propositions that are empirically testable and those who perceive the extant theory and knowledge base to be too weak to justify such limitation. The latter approach often produces "rich" descriptions of individual situations and the accompanying hope is that commonalities will emerge as the number of cases so examined grows. Almost paradoxically, as the knowledge base has grown so has the realisation that a host of the key issues are very difficult to address within a purely scientific frame, no matter what the methodology; common sense, logic, and the wisdom of practitioners come to the fore as important sources of knowledge in their own right.

A classification of the research

At the risk of oversimplification, the research literature can be organised into four categories. Very approximately, these categories correspond to their chronological emergence in the literature, although there is considerable overlap in subject and time, and work in all areas continues. The four categories are:

a) *Research on teacher characteristics*: the defining purpose of this area has been to discover those stable characteristics of teachers such as sex, verbal fluency, teacher training, and experience which correlate with student outcomes.

b) *Research on teaching strategies*: Research in this category addresses the effectiveness of teaching approaches that can be generalised beyond any specific contents or curriculum area. This strand can in turn be sub-divided:

    i) **Process-product research**: The principal aim here is to seek specific teaching behaviours that are related to student achievement. The focus is thus away from fixed characteristics of teachers and towards aspects of teaching itself that are alterable and amenable to development through appropriate teacher education and other policies.

    ii) **Wholistic teaching strategies**: Research in this case concentrates on general approaches to teaching and organising classrooms. Typically, the strategies examined are familiar to practicing teachers with additional theoretical support from sociological or psychological research. The strategies reported below are those which have some demonstrated effectiveness such as peer tutoring, mastery learning, and cooperative learning.

c) *Teaching special populations*: Over the past twenty years or so, considerable attention has been given to the teaching of special populations of children such as the disadvantaged, bilingual, handicapped, and gifted. Much of the early work in this category adopted behaviourist and individual differences psychology, but more recently the theoretical underpinnings have spread to linguistics and the cognitive sciences.

d) *Teacher competency research*. This work on teaching is relatively recent and integrates three strands by examining: pedagogy within content areas, the influence of context in teaching, and the different ways in which teachers' thought processes influence their work.

a) *Research on teacher characteristics*

This became a prominent area in the mid-1960s with the publication of the Coleman report, results from Project Talent, and the early studies conducted by the International Association for the Evaluation of Educational Achievement (IEA)[3]. Each of these was based on large-scale surveys of pupils, schools, and teachers and hence examined existing, naturally-occurring patterns and outcomes, rather than experimental data. The main elements of schooling that were deemed in need of explanation and by which it should be judged were student outcomes as represented by standardized measures of academic achievement, while the principal explanatory variables were measures of teacher and school characteristics. Variants of correlation and regression analysis were deployed, the assumption being that well-specified equations (i.e. models of the schooling process) would permit the estimation of the "true" effects of the different factors, such as teacher's prior experience or type of training, on pupil results. The Coleman study remains probably the best-known work in this category, making a substantial impact at the time of its publication and generating a number of more recent "offspring" reports[4].

Despite its prominence, the early work did lack sophistication. For one thing, almost all such studies collected school-wide data on teachers, students, and their environments, thereby averaging out and comparing characteristics of whole schools rather than seeking

71

to associate *individual* teachers and their characteristics with the observed outcomes of their students. That is, they examined the relationship between one school average, say, "teacher years of experience," and another school average "student achievement score", not that between, for instance, a specific teacher's experience and the results of the pupils in his or her charge. A further shortcoming was that most of the earlier studies were conducted at only one point in time, rather than encompassing change over time, which thereby reduced the possibility of achieving adequately specified equations. Though later studies did not overcome all of the methodological shortcomings, certain of them did include measures of student achievement taken at two or more points in time and some sought to link individual teachers to students[5].

Two main sets of findings have emerged from this set of studies which have been summarised by Hanushek[6]. First, other factors (such as social background) being equal, most of the variation in students' achievement lies *within* rather than *among* schools. Put another way, the differences among the achievement scores of students within a school tend to be almost as large as the differences in those among students in the system overall. Not surprisingly, therefore, these studies have been able to find few characteristics of schools or characteristics of the teachers within them that, on average, regularly relate to the average achievement of the students[7]. Insofar as the surveys have been able to measure them, the characteristics of schools that appear to be neutral with respect to student achievement include the level of school expenditure, library facilities, the existence and quality of science laboratories, age and quality of the school building, the average age, salary, educational background, teaching experience, verbal ability and sex of teachers, among others, operationalised in relatively simple fashion to make them amenable to the large-scale survey instrument. There is some indication, however, that students in schools where teachers have high average verbal scores do better than students in other schools, but the relationship is weak and erratic[8]. There also is increasing evidence from within this research tradition that certain aspects of school organisation that can be measured by surveys have a consistent relationship to school-wide student achievement. These include the purposive nature of the institution towards improving academic results, a positive climate, shared decision-making by the staff, and a safe school environment[9].

Second, although the variation among schools is relatively small, there is considerable variation in student achievement *between classes* within schools. This may suggest that there are significant differences in the capacity of teachers to improve results, as measured by student achievement test scores, although an alternative or complementary explanation is that students of different ability are systematically assigned to different groupings[10]. Unfortunately, as seen, few studies actually link students to teachers to enable assessments to be made of the relationship between individual teacher characteristics and student achievement. In those that do allow some such comparisons, none of the usual list of observed teacher characteristics – educational experiences and background, salary, verbal test scores, sex, age, and years of teaching experience – shows a regular, significant effect on measured student achievement, though the verbal scores of teachers and the years of teaching experience do show up positively in a few studies[11]. One reason for the lack of strong relationships may be that teachers vary in their success in raising achievement levels from year to year; investigations of how well teachers do across time have found only modest stability[12]. This does not mean that some teachers are not regularly more or less effective than others; it does suggest that most vary in their effectiveness as this is indicated, to repeat, by the criterion of measured test scores.

On the whole, therefore, the conclusions that emerged from this tradition were weak or negative, casting some doubt on the common-sense notion of the "good" teacher as an invaluable educational resource. As emphasized, however, the design of the studies included in this category were not generally conducive to the direct identification of who that "good" teacher is or what effective teaching might be. Other research provided grounds for greater optimism.

b) Research on teaching strategies

Partially in response to the generally negative conclusions of the research on teacher characteristics and to the finding that teachers vary in their effectiveness, investigators in the late 1960s and early 1970s began to explore more thoroughly the actual process of teaching. Whereas the principal disciplines informing the former body of work were sociology and economics, this brand of research instead drew heavily on psychology. Two promising strands belong here, having at least two main features in common but differing on another. Both focus on teaching strategies within classrooms and both are independent of the content or curriculum being taught. One (process-product research) focuses on discrete teaching activities and behaviours, and patterns of these, that correlate with student achievement. The other analyses general teaching techniques such as co-operative learning, mastery learning, and peer and cross-age tutoring (wholistic teacher strategies).

i) Process-product research

The label accurately defines the dimensions: the optic is the classroom, the *process* of teaching involves the observed behaviour and interactions of students and teachers, and the *product* is the short- and long-term growth of pupils and students, variously measured. The main early methodology was to observe classrooms closely and the observations were then classified into different categories of what teachers and students do. The frequency of their occurrence was then related to student outcomes in the hope of finding stable relationships[13].Originally, this work concentrated on a variety of very specific behaviours such as the nature of questioning adopted by the teacher, the presentation of materials organised in advance, the use and types of positive reinforcement and the types of feedback given by teachers to different student actions.

As the work progressed, it became more sophisticated. It sought to combine the discrete aspects of teaching, to explore curvilinear relationships, and to replicate findings[14]. Distinctions came to be drawn between types of classroom behaviours, not just specific practices. For example, some activities appeared to be important to classroom management and through that indirectly to student achievement; others related directly to learning. Finally, researchers such as Brophy and Good put together patterns of variables associated with what seemed to be effective teaching. These patterns were constructed from independent correlations and were not actually representative of any individual's teaching. In general, effective teaching was seen to involve the active interaction between the teacher and students, the optimisation of academic learning time, the rewarding of achievement, high expectations, and well organised and structured presentations of content[15]. Of course, much of this might be obvious to the practised teacher. The value of this work was the provision of empirical support to the insight of the practitioner.

Once relatively solid patterns had been established, each of which correlated with measures of student achievement, work in this research tradition made the major step forward of trying them out experimentally. If teachers could learn and be trained to behave in "effective" ways and if this in turn increased the achievement of their students, the power of this approach would lie in moving from a more systematic understanding of what goes into good teaching towards the more widespread adoption of these practices.

By and large, the findings are positive and impressive[16]. In most of the experiments, teachers trained in "effective" strategies increased student achievement more than those who continued as before. Two of the primary investigators in the field, Brophy and Good, felt confident to conclude:

"Most findings must be qualified by grade level, type of objective, type of student, and other context factors. This creates dilemmas for teachers working with heterogeneous classes. Furthermore, even within context, it seems likely that all relationships are ultimately curvilinear. Too much of even a generally good thing is still too much.

At least two common themes cut across the findings, despite the need for limitations and qualifications. One is that academic learning is influenced by the amount of time that students spend engaged in appropriate learning tasks. The second is that students learn more effectively when their teachers first structure new information for them and help them relate it to what they already know, and then monitor their performance and provide corrective feedback during recitation, drill, practice, or application activities. For a time, these generalisations seemed confined to the early grades or to basic rather than more advanced skills. However, it now appears that they apply to any body of knowledge or set of skills that has been sufficiently well organised and analysed so that it can be presented (explained, modeled) systematically and then practiced or applied during activities that call for student performance that can be evaluated for quality and (where incorrect or imperfect) given corrective feedback" (p. 366).

While there may well be greater limits to the generalisability of the findings than Brophy and Good wish to suggest, it represents the careful and focused application of observation and replication to the actual activity of teaching.

ii) Wholistic teaching approaches

Whereas the process-product work starts from the identification of individual, "effective" teaching behaviours as a means of developing more coherent instructional strategies, the wholistic tradition within this category starts out from a coherent conception of a teaching strategy, derived either from observation or from theory. Over the past twenty years, a variety of such strategies have been developed and evaluated. As with the process-product work, the strategies in this category are largely independent of the actual subject matter to be taught.

Individualised instruction is an approach that was especially popular in the 1960s and 1970s. It builds on the incontrovertible premise that children differ in their learning aptitudes and styles. A second, more specific premise is that learning, no matter how complex the subject, rests on the acquisition of a sequence of less complex components. Application of this latter idea provides a powerful link to the first: if the knowledge and skills needed by a student can be broken down into ordered, discrete parts, then progress can be much more easily monitored. Among the earlier examples here from the 1960s was B.F. Skinner's programmed instruction, which sought to marry the individualisation of learning with technology. Other major curriculum efforts included "Individually Prescribed Instruction" (IPI) developed at the University of Pittsburgh, and "Individually Guided Education" (IGE) developed at the University of Wisconsin. After the initial enthusiasm, each has tended to disappear, due in part to evaluations that found that they were not more successful than other forms of instruction and in part to problems of implementation and technological constraints[17].

Their most popular successor was *mastery learning*, which can be used either for individual pupils or, more commonly, as a group-based approach in conventional classrooms. Based on Carroll's model and on later work by Bloom, the basic tenet of mastery learning is again simple: virtually all students – say, 19 out of every 20 – can master a basic curriculum if given sufficient time and proper instruction[18]. Mastery learning programmes are characterised too by clearly-defined learning objectives that are broken down into small discrete units, each with an established criterion level of performance or "mastery". These are organised hierarchically so that successful mastery of initial units is required before students can proceed to the more complex ones. Mastery learning relies on frequent pupil assessment through formative tests with specific instruction for those adjudged deficient in order to rectify their lack[19].

Claims of the substantial effectiveness of this approach have been largely based on short-term, small-scale experiments, many of which have major methodological flaws[20]. There is little evidence of sustained effects over time, nor is there strong empirical support for the rigidly hierarchical nature of many mastery learning models[21]. Critics have charged that many such programmes are too structured and mechanistic, and overly focused on minute basic skills to the neglect of broader curricular concerns or higher-order thinking skills. In part, this could be only a matter of overcoming practical difficulties of implementation. Even then there remain substantial problems: first, of determining the "correct" order by which to sequence the learning and, second, of presenting to very *different* children, all learning at different speeds, the *same* material in approximately the same order. The criticisms mentioned above certainly found public voice when the Chicago Mastery Learning Reading Program, mandated citywide, was discontinued in 1985 when parents took legal action arguing that it was ill-designed and fragmented and not actually teaching their children to read with comprehension[22].

A second approach within this category is that based on *structured student interactions*. A rich literature has built up on the positive learning effects of small group interactions and of peers working in pairs and groups, leading to the development, over the last thirty years or so, of specific strategies for peer and cross-age tutoring and small group, co-operative learning. These are among the most thoroughly researched and regularly most effective approaches for certain kinds of learning. Probably the most widely used of these are student tutoring methods, involving either students of the same age who have already mastered the skill being taught (peer tutoring) or older students teaching their juniors (cross-age tutoring). Both can be employed to supplement the often scarce amount of teacher time available for the lower achieving students. A recent analysis of 65 studies of peer and cross-age tutoring, for instance, found that they had positive effects on the academic performance and attitudes of both the student tutees and tutors alike amounting to an average effect size on academic performance of 0.40 of a standard deviation for those being tutored and of 0.33 of a standard deviation for those serving as the tutors[23]. The effects were largest in well-structured programmes and in mathematics, but less in reading. One reason for such positive results may be the increases in the proportion of time that students are actively engaged in academic tasks, whether the youngster is attempting to learn or to teach[24].

Closely akin to peer tutoring is *co-operative learning*. In many of the models based on this, groups of 4 to 6 students work together on a given task, with the reward or assessment being determined on the basis of the group's performance rather than, or in addition to, that of the individual pupil. Proponents argue that this "team" approach has several important benefits in terms of raising appreciation both of achievement and co-operation, of enhanced motivation (especially for weaker pupils), and of, in some circumstances, allowing genuine multicultural co-operation in ways that may have wider application to other policies involving target groups of students[25]. Reviews have indeed found significant positive effects on academic and attitudinal measures in well-designed studies. The degree of effectiveness, however, appears to be mediated by such factors as the composition of the group, the degree of structure in and clarity of objectives, the subject matter, and the reward system[26].

Together, wholistic teaching approaches provide an interesting and still developing field, yielding some very positive results depending on the area of application and the nature of implementation. They have drawn fruitfully on a range of disciplines and insights, often adopting the same principles as in the *process-product* work, namely: maximisation of learning time, interactive instruction (through using peers), and high expectations for students manifested through giving them more autonomy. The nature and practicalities of implementation are, however, critical to success. Without adequate organisation of the classroom, reorganisation of the school, sufficient teaching resources to meet problems of noise and stress, and proper training and retraining, they can fall to the ground. Finally, it should be emphasized that, as with most reforms, there is considerable potential for distortion when these strategies are implemented from a top-down mandate, that loses sight of the original aims and value. This was precisely the criticism concerning the Chicago Mastery Learning Reading Program referred to above. The central administration may set direction, establish content frameworks, and give assistance, but it should not rigidly mandate specific instructional strategies that depend on active co-operation and development within schools, by teachers and pupils.

c) Teaching special populations

Teachers and schools are today called on to meet the needs of an increasingly diverse population of students. Certain of the policy implications of this demand, as they relate to specific sections of the student population, will be elaborated in the following chapter. They represent some of the most demanding of the "new tasks and challenges" that have been added to the modern teacher's agenda. But the fact of teaching an increasingly diverse student body, and the experience of specifically-designed programmes for new priority groups in education, have also given rise to their own body of literature. As yet, however, it is a field with a powerful and rich conceptual base but frustratingly few consistent and replicable findings. At the risk of complicating still further our classification scheme, this body of research can also be divided into two sub-categories.

i) Aptitude-treatment interaction research (ATI)

This is based on the simple insight that given approaches to teaching and learning have different effects on different pupils and students. Students differ in their aptitudes and teaching approaches differ in the demands they make in return[27]. Despite the lack of consistency of results, one general pattern that does emerge in the literature is that students with low ability or motivation seem to require instruction that *mediates* their understanding and learning. Integrating the findings on ATI with those on teaching effectiveness, Peterson[28] draws the following conclusions, emphasizing the commonalities as well as differences among learners:

- *All* pupils actively construct meaning when they learn. Effective teaching should emphasize higher-order as well as lower-order thinking for both the gifted and the slow learner. This is especially important for the low-achieving students, who have more difficulty developing higher-order thinking skills by themselves.

76

- The effects of increasing instructional time interact with the level and type of prior achievement; the *quality* of time devoted to learning is often more important for the low-achieving students and for higher-order learning than is the sheer *quantity* of time.
- Direct instruction, which is particularly effective for low-ability students, is a necessary but not sufficient method for teaching higher-order skills to any student, whether high- or low-achieving. It needs to be combined with other more open-ended strategies in order to foster both knowledge construction and the understanding of students of when and how to apply their knowledge and skills.
- Students should have the opportunity to participate in small heterogeneous ability groups which, as discussed above, can foster both achievement and motivation.
- The teaching of actual *thinking skills* can be particularly useful for low-aptitude students by providing them with the cognitive strategies they would not otherwise have developed on their own.

ii) The study of cultural differences

This body of research on teaching special populations focuses on *cultural differences* among students and how these affect school success. Many such studies identify a mismatch between the cultural/linguistic patterns or expectations of the school and teacher and those of some or all of the students. Many also draw attention to the influence of the social and cultural context in which the education takes place, and how this affects learning and teaching[29].

The shortcoming of much of the ethnographic research included here is its lack of generalisability to other situations and hence the difficulty of using the findings as the basis for policy changes. Also, much of it is concerned exclusively with the interactions taking place in the classroom, making it extremely difficult to draw the connection with the actual content of what is being taught[30]. Recognising these difficulties, Tharpe has elaborated a number of lessons that emerge from this research[31]. He suggests that all teaching for underachieving or disadvantaged cultural groups should place special emphasis on language development. It should alternate between and integrate school concepts, on the one hand, and the everyday experiences of the students, on the other. In addition to these "constants", the variable conditions and cultures of different groups will necessitate adaptability in the classroom in terms of motivational techniques, the organisation of groupings and the classroom, sociolinguistic conventions, and cognitive organisation patterns that are consistent with the cultural experience of the students. This, of course, makes the major assumptions that the school and the teacher are familiar with these to start with, which is a requirement, if met, with clear implications for both teacher training (in-service as well as pre-service) and selection.

This body of research lacks precise policy implications for two reasons. First, it has generated few consistent replicable findings. Second, in its emphasis on the need to recognise both differences and similarities between pupils and their learning needs, it renders problematic the identification of straightforward conclusions. It highlights the range of cultural, linguistic, and aptitude differences of students, and corresponding pedagogical strategies to meet these, which have potentially far-reaching implications for teacher education. But much of this research also recognises the commonalities of the teaching and learning needs of all children[32]. Brophy summarises it thus:

"Research has turned up very little evidence suggesting the need for *qualitatively* different forms of instruction for students who differ in aptitude, achievement level, socioeconomic status, ethnicity, or learning style. Main effects tend to be much more frequent and powerful than interactions, and the interactions that do occur tend to be ordinal interactions indicating that some students need more (of the same kind of) instruction rather than disordinal interactions indicating that some students need to' be taught one way but other students need to be taught a different way"[33].

The conclusion here is that teachers need to have a broad repertoire of strategies and be able to decide when and how much of any one of them to use with any given child. Even without taking all the other demands on teachers into account, this research on special populations points up the high levels of professional skills required: being sensitive to a myriad of student differences in background and aptitude, up to date on the different strategies that might prove most effective for each, and skilled in applying these in ways that together still constitute a coherent, lively learning environment for all. Apart from any "new" tasks and challenges as discussed in the next chapter, the long-standing challenge of bringing along each child to the best of his or her abilities is alone an infinitely demanding one.

Furthermore, while more homogeneous ability groupings of pupils may facilitate the task of the teacher, they are not necessarily in the best interests of the children. Heterogeneity in classrooms can have positive effects on student learning, motivation, and social developments. Conversely, homogeneity of student groups – based either on ethnicity or aptitude – can sometimes be more detrimental than helpful. Where children are withdrawn from their regular classroom for special instruction or offered materials that break down tasks into small isolated units, the result is often the fragmentation of learning, emphasis on the rote learning of isolated skills, lower exposure to broad areas of curriculum, and the reduced fostering of comprehension and higher-order thinking. This is especially detrimental for low ability children because they in particular need more help in drawing connections between different items of information or skills[34]. It is impossible to generalise here about the overall merits and problems with mixed ability classes *versus* different types of organisation that use selection, except to underline that strategies that serve to isolate children from peers or that fragment learning are unlikely to be a success.

d) Teacher competency research

Teacher competency research shows promise in deepening our understanding of how to improve teaching by shifting the emphasis of enquiry from the behaviour and activity of teachers and students to actual thinking and learning, that is, the cognitive determinants of that behaviour[35]. Three recent lines of enquiry are relevant here.

The first of these examines *how students process, integrate, remember, and use new information.* One line of this particular field of study is characterised by carefully conducted studies of specific learning tasks, such as simple division and algebraic word problems in mathematics, and understanding single sentences and simple paragraphs in reading. One outcome of this work has been the documentation of the interactionist nature of learning; it requires the active engagement by the student with the content. Another branch within this first field of enquiry has analysed expertise for a complex task (such as chess playing or solving a physics problem) and compared it with the efforts of a novice confronting a similar task. A further area of exploration has been into the nature of the naïve understanding of scientific concepts and the ways in which people, both young and old, hold to these even in the face of evidence and teaching to the contrary.

One key idea that emerges from all this is that it is impossible clearly to separate complex ("higher order") from simple ("lower order") learning tasks[36] and this suggests that the common distinction between the teaching of basic skills and of problem-solving is artificial and may ultimately be damaging. The teacher in the early (and later) grades who unduly emphasizes the drill and practice of skills and the memorisation of algorithms may well be doing his or her students a disservice. The complexity of a learning task depends upon the level of initial knowledge of the learner in the subject area. A complex task for a novice will be simple for an expert – the more a student learns about a subject, the more complex a task must be for it to require complex thinking. This suggests that greater depth, rather than broad coverage, is required if the curriculum is to stimulate higher-order thinking. This strand of research strongly supports emphasis on the need for teachers to have a very sound grounding in their particular academic disciplines.

The second area of study under this broad heading of teacher competency research focuses on the *thought processes of teachers* – their theories and beliefs, their methods of planning, and their strategies of decision-making. Its roots are shared between the influential earlier book, *Life in Classrooms* (1968) by Philip Jackson, and the work of cognitive scientists on understanding thinking behaviour[37]. The field is young but it has already generated considerable attention and some consistent findings. In their recent comprehensive review, Clark and Peterson conclude that the research evidence supports an image of teaching as a complex, cognitively demanding enterprise and of the teacher as a reflective professional much like a physician or lawyer. Another set of findings identifies the interactive nature of the teaching process in that teachers constantly and actively attend to the complexities of classroom interactions, making on-the-spot decisions at a rate, on average, of once every two minutes. While these decisions are based primarily on judgements about the learners, teachers respond to a variety of other contextual factors as well. A further object of study are teachers' theories and beliefs regarding the teaching/learning process, the abilities of their students, and the content of instruction. The conclusion here seems to be that even homogeneous groups of teachers vary widely in the content and orientation of their implicit theories but that the correspondence between these theories and teachers' classroom behaviour is often moderated by circumstances beyond their control[38].

Though this second area of research is new and still developing, the consistency and intuitive logic of some of these findings suggest several practical conclusions. One is the importance of in-service and supervised training experiences for improving the quality of teaching and for developing an explicit set of theories and beliefs about the process of teaching. In addition, the emerging picture of teachers as reflective professionals underscores the need for the culture and policies of the school to support the work of the teaching staff, through allocation of time for planning, opportunities for collaboration and professional growth, and so forth. Finally, the emphasis in this work on the importance of teachers having a good understanding both of the content of their discipline and of the pedagogy for teaching is that it reinforces the findings from the cognitive studies of students about the need for strong training in the discipline in the pre-service years.

The third and final main direction of this area of educational enquiry focuses on *teaching within the content areas*. This field too is diverse and in some respects new. Suffice it to say here that it breaks down the teacher's knowledge of content into the different categories of subject-matter knowledge, pedagogical knowledge within the subject area, and curricular knowledge. The main question that is posed in this case is not whether it is necessary to use "hands-on" methods to teach science or some other method, but rather what kinds of subject matter and pedagogical skills are necessary for a teacher to do a good job of teaching science or any other subject[39].

Some lessons to be drawn

This review, necessarily selective and organised according to one particular classification system, points up a number of main conclusions. First, educational research is producing a large body of valuable work, with fresh discovery and new domains. Obviously, that conclusion would be reinforced were all OECD countries to be embraced in a single review. But, second (and perhaps as a direct result of the growth and diversification of this research), there are many areas where scientific enquiries offer interesting insights and potentially fruitful avenues for further study but relatively few unequivocally firm conclusions on which to base policies. And that is not only because of the incompleteness of research enquiry in any particular field; it is also because the infinitely complex and ever-changing world can never be fully grasped and reduced to a researcher's model. And there are always political choices to be made that research cannot resolve one way or the other; they require the application of fundamental values. But however incomplete the relationship between research and action, it is important, wherever possible, to clarify the limits of ignorance and to eliminate hypotheses and practices known to have failed. Finally, this review has shown how incomplete were the questions and methodologies of the "teacher characteristics" research that helped to fuel the pessimism of the 1970s. Continuing enquiry, as well as common sense and educational wisdom, has counterbalanced the sway of a tradition that was able to ask "Do teachers make a difference?". They do.

TEACHER EDUCATION AND TRAINING

Conflicting conclusions from the research

One difficulty in drawing direct implications from the research surveyed concerning teacher education is that it can be used to support contradictory conclusions. The generally negative conclusion of the teacher characteristics literature is that few consistent relationships between different aspects of the education and training of the profession and student achievement can be identified. This has been interpreted by some as suggesting that research provides no clear support for proposals that prospective teachers need either a certain high minimum level of initial education or carefully designed programmes covering subject knowledge or pedagogy and practice. (Although this type of study addresses differential not absolute effects, *reductio ad absurdum*, it comes perilously near to doubting the value of any teacher preparation whatever). In contrast, the teacher competency research strongly supports the need for a sound grounding in the subject matter to be taught, while the literature on teaching strategies and special populations attest to the importance of a very good command of pedagogical knowledge and techniques.

This discrepancy between the different traditions may partly be only a matter of research design. The criterion of "measured student achievement" represents a decidedly limited criterion by which to judge good teaching and the preparation of the profession, both in principle and especially in its operational measurement through standardized pupil test scores. The measures used by the characteristics research to distinguish the different types of preparation that teachers have received in terms of the quality, duration, and relevance of teacher training have often been patently crude and inadequate.

But the discrepancy between the conclusions of the different strands of research may also derive from educational realities, not methodological factors, in ways that take the matter out of the arcane world of academic argument and into the policy realm. That is, if insufficient numbers of teachers and schools are applying the rich répertoire of teaching skills on the basis of a full and varied curriculum once they begin in the classroom but are concentrating instead on the "basics" and memorisation, then differences in the quality of teacher education will show up little in pupils' results. Moreover, if many teacher education programmes are in fact of a disappointing quality, then the characteristics work has actually uncovered a worrying empirical reality, namely that attendance at one or another such programme makes little discernible difference to pupils' results. A propos of this, as Smith and O'Day themselves assess the situation:

> "In the U.S. the quality of pre-service training is monitored by the individual institutions, by a non-government accreditation board (NCATE), and by the states. Standards have varied and are generally low"[40].

Generally, the extensive attention devoted over the years to the improvement of teacher education, especially pre-service, even by those whose support of education is generous and optimistic, suggests this concern to be widely shared. It in turn suggests a shift in emphasis away from paramount attention to the quality of the student intake to education courses towards a strong additional concern for the adequacy of the teacher training programmes being provided. It is that concern which lay behind the establishment of, for instance, the Council for the Accreditation of Teacher Education (CATE) in the United Kingdom in 1984[41].

Yet insofar as mediocre teacher education is a reality, it should be noted in defence of present staff that research conducted in the 1960s and early 1970s, that could find few measurable characteristics of teachers that positively enhanced student achievement at that time, was actually to enquire into the durable effects of teacher training delivered at any time from before World War II up to the mid-1960s, not current preparation. Whatever the assessment of current teacher education programmes, this research casts doubt, if anything, on the quality of the very past provision that the critics often pronounce so favourably on.

In fact, the different schools of research reviewed possess a different focus of enquiry. The teacher characteristics research attempts to describe and account for the overall picture while the other strands concentrate on identifying and generalising good practice. To discover that in the aggregate there are only weak correlations between certain aspects of teacher training and desired educational outcomes, far from supporting the contention that teacher education "doesn't matter", suggests it should receive even greater priority.

Knowledge of subject matter

The above review of the recent research literature and the force of logic both support the need for entering teachers to possess a good command of subject matter. Both depth and breadth of knowledge in a content area are critical for those entrusted with giving students the opportunity to engage in complex cognitive activities. How the standards required should be defined is not clear cut, however, and the results of the teacher characteristics studies suggest caution in pinning hope on easy answers. More accreditation visits to education faculties, now commonly seen in the United States, and more required courses in order to be qualified, however useful, provide only a partial answer. Requiring a bachelor's degree in a relevant discipline supports the need for breadth and depth but does not guarantee that a middle or secondary school teacher will be familiar with the material to be covered in their particular assignments, even when it is in the same area. And the mere possession of an undergraduate degree does not begin to address the content needs of the primary school teacher single-handedly responsible for a wide curriculum, although it may give some indication of the ability to go in a certain depth into a particular field. The question here is at least twofold: what sort of mastery of subject matter does any particular undergraduate degree equip the prospective teacher with, and can this be translated by the teacher to unfamiliar topics that broadly apply the same principles of knowledge that the univerity qualification has conveyed?

The problems are, if anything, exacerbated for already-practising teachers. Disciplinary knowledge has grown and evolved over the years, particularly in the sciences, reading (linguistics, cognitive science, and developmental psychology), history and social studies (sociology, economics), and mathematics. The need to keep abreast of these developments implies high quality continuing professional development. Yet, our reviewers of research and policy in the United States go as far as to assert that, for that country at least: "current in-service teacher education may be the weakest link in the entire educational enterprise". The importance of in-service education and training (INSET) for all OECD countries recurs throughout this report. As seen below, even where the level and organisation of INSET remains palpably inadequate for the educational challenges of today, many OECD countries have moved significantly towards recognising that importance. Yet precisely because of the changes in knowledge as well as in school curricula, quite apart from other influential factors such as the ageing of the teaching force, the task of organising and delivering in-service education is a never-ending one. In other words, a short-term drive for its improvement must be sustained in order to be effective. INSET is a high and permanent priority.

The implied need that emerges from the research and the foregoing discussion for teachers to be both well-grounded in the specific content they are responsible for as well as generally competent in a discipline – a need that can be more readily applied in the case of secondary level subject teachers than to the generalist at the primary level, whatever his or her specialism – is a reminder that simply ensuring that teachers possess certain qualifications is far from a sufficient condition of good teaching. In this section, concerned as it is with knowledge of subject matter rather than pedagogical or organisational skills, this implies, at the least, that the teacher's knowledge is actually relevant to the subject matter to be taught. The public debate has often tended to focus on the background qualifications of new teachers to the relative neglect of the relevance of those qualifications to classroom teaching, quite apart from the actual quality of either their pre-service or the in-service training. A number of OECD countries are currently seeking to rectify that imbalance. It suggests too that teacher training policies should be well co-ordinated, where possible, with those for the curriculum. A major difficulty arises here, particularly for pre-service teacher education, when the curriculum is subject to ever-more rapid change. This source of change is both an outstanding challenge and potentially burdensome for teachers today, and is taken up in greater detail in the following chapter. One anomaly witnessed in many countries is that one of the sectors that has most to struggle to ensure proper recognition of its programmes and its students' achievements – the vocational sector – is among the most stringent in requiring that the teachers and trainees are well prepared in the actual subject matter to be taught.

Pedagogical training and educational understanding

While few dissent from the need for teachers to have a firm foundation of knowledge, even if that base is not easy to define for many teachers, there is far less consensus about the importance of pedagogical training and the understanding of pupils and their learning. There is a common, misguided viewpoint that anyone with sufficient knowledge of a subject can teach it. This is being translated into practice in some states of the United States, report Smith and O'Day, through the adoption of policies whereby prospective teachers earn an undergraduate degree with a disciplinary major and then gain on-the-job experience in schools with very little pedagogical training. They describe the general thrust of current developments in that country to be away from requiring more or different pre- or in-service teacher training in pedagogical and psychological areas[42].This tendency may be present in many of the initiatives now emerging, as described above, to encourage the entry of new teachers from non-traditional backgrounds into the education system whether on the grounds that these entrants enhance the overall quality of the teaching force, or that they represent much-needed "new blood" with diverse knowledge and experience of relevance to the modern curriculum, or that they serve to alleviate problems of supply, or combinations of all three. The research surveyed suggests extreme caution in assuming that a firm emphasis on mastery of subject matter is to be encouraged *at the expense* of pedagogical and teaching skills.

First, studies into teacher thinking underscore the false nature of the sharp dichotomy between content and pedagogical/psychological knowledge for teaching. Teachers need a répertoire of teaching strategies that are embedded deeply in content areas. Second, the results of experimental studies on generic teaching strategies are promising enough to suggest that they themselves be included in pre-service and in-service training for teachers of appropriate subjects. Teachers could usefully be made aware of the strengths and weaknesses of various research-based teaching strategies that have been shown to be effective in certain situations. This would encourage, for example, teachers to have "active" teaching strategies in their répertoires. Teachers at all levels could benefit from at least familiarity with methodologies like mastery learning, peer and cross-age tutoring, and co-operative and group learning and be cognisant of when to employ them. Moreover, new entrants to the profession should understand the institutional constraints in implementing some of these approaches in order to avoid their mechanistic application with possibly undesirable side effects. Not all schools or communities can accept the disruption that peer tutoring, some forms of group learning, and strategies designed to engage pupils in active problem-solving, entail. Third, the research on teaching special populations argues for teachers to be aware of individual differences they are likely to encounter among their students and of appropriate pedagogical strategies for addressing them.

Some policy developments

Actual policy developments across a wide range of the OECD countries display certain trends that are broadly consistent with the directions suggested by the research. For example, the sheer length of teacher preparation has been generally extended, though not necessarily in both subject preparation and pedagogical training, nor have the changes been uniform across OECD countries. For this report, global trends in pre- and in-service teacher education can best be summarised by reference to recent international reviews[43,44], here quoting from Neave's synthesis prepared for the Council of Europe:

> "Developments that have also been noted in connection with pre-primary training are also discernible at the primary level – affiliation of Colleges of Education to universities in Ireland, the partial linkage between the "Ecoles Normales" and the university in training of primary school teachers in France and the extension of course length from

83

four semesters to six in Austria with analogous moves in Finland (four years to five), France (from two years post-Baccalauréat to three in 1979, followed in 1986 by two years study at university), Ireland (two year courses extended to three in 1975), Luxembourg (two to three in 1983) and, in certain parts of Switzerland where teacher education is carried out in normal schools, the period under training was extended from four to six years. Similarly, in Portugal, time under training was raised from two to three years in 1976, followed in 1985 by placing three-year courses in Higher Schools of Education" (p. 9)[43].

The CERI (Centre for Educational Research and Innovation) review of trends in teacher training[44] notes that for teachers in secondary education, the question of how long their total training should last, including the professional/pedagogical component, remains an open one. From many quarters, there have been recommendations that it should be extended with particular emphasis on preparation for teaching in classrooms, including the ability to relate school learning to developments in the world outside. Current shortages of applicants may be discouraging certain authorities and institutions from taking full note of these recommendations.

Detailed information on INSET, as with in-service education and training in other occupational fields outside teaching, is notoriously difficult to come by. Much of it takes place in non-formal settings or in schools and colleges themselves. Much is of a short-term nature. There is diversity of organising authority. For all these reasons, statistics are lacking though they could doubtless be improved. Indeed, as the quality of the teaching force, and hence their preparation, especially in-service, becomes a national priority in many countries, it is difficult to envisage how improvements can be made without more comprehensive information about and coherent policies towards INSET. Progress is nevertheless apparent, as Neave reports:

"Earlier in this analysis, it was suggested that one of the outstanding developments of the decade was the growth of in-service teacher education. Indeed, as the number of newly fledged teachers taking up post falls – as it has done over the past half decade in most countries – the price of meeting change in mission and knowledge, skills and qualifications has to be paid by quite massive expansion in this area. Some countries already have in place extensive systems of in-service teaching. In Denmark, for instance, around 30 per cent of pre-primary school staff attend at least one course per year, whilst, due to limitation on places, only 20 per cent of teachers in the *Folkeskole* are admitted per year to part-time courses. Other countries, no less ambitious, are gearing up both provision and facilities to deal with a very substantial percentage of their teaching body per year. Italy has set the annual target at 30 per cent of the whole teaching profession participating per annum. Similar priorities are to be seen in France.... Likewise, in the Netherlands, plans envisage some 40 000 teachers undergoing in-service education. These figures speak for themselves. They show very clearly the high priority governments everywhere place upon this aspect of teacher formation" (p. 17)[43].

There remain, nonetheless, marked differences of country practices and behind the raw figures lie the outstanding questions of the quality and relevance of the courses provided for prospective and practising teachers. Some countries report the requirement for extensive proportions of teacher preparation to be devoted to the pedagogical aspects of their future work. This comprises about a fifth to a quarter of the credits to be earned during the 5-6 years needed in Finland to become a specialist subject teacher which stands in marked contrast with, for instance, Greece where possession of a university or equivalent degree alone is sufficient in order to be such a teacher[45].

No less are there marked contrasts concerning the time devoted to teaching practice as an element of pre-service preparation either as an integral part of the programme or as a fully-fledged induction period. In some, teacher preparation is still a predominantly academic exercise with little sustained experience of the school situation. Others have followed a quite different path. In Germany, for example, teaching practice has long been so fully integrated into initial teacher education that the probationary period or *Referendarzeit*, which lasts from 18 months to 2 years, involves teaching under supervision and course work, and full teacher status is only achieved on completion of a second state examination (*zweites Staatsexamen*) at the end of the probationary period[46].

There are then a number of countries where the tendency is counter to that reported for the United States and where the pedagogical component of training for secondary teachers is being assigned greater importance. This reflects the perception that preparation that is too academic is unlikely to be sufficiently attuned to the needs of students and schools. The reforms of the preparation of upper secondary teachers in the Netherlands, for instance, have meant the reduction of academic study from 6 to 4 years, the introduction of a follow-on one-year course leading to qualification, of which at least half is devoted to teaching practice[43].

The foregoing review of the research literature has suggested the need for staff to possess a good foundation in the fields that they are to teach and to be knowledgeable of pedagogical theories and techniques that are grounded in those fields. This raises the question of coherence between teacher training and the organisation of the education system as a whole. In the Scandinavian countries of Denmark and Sweden in particular, a major direction of reform for the compulsory school years has lain in reducing the rigid divides between the primary and secondary school years. In some, too, such as the Netherlands, greater integration has been sought between the pre-primary and primary levels. In many countries, developments in vocational education have been typified by the introduction of a greater degree of theory and general content[47], though not necessarily to be taught by the same teachers. Given these changes, it is reasonable to conclude that the requirement for a teacher to possess specialist knowledge linked to the age of the student and subject matter to be taught becomes the more demanding, the wider is the teacher's brief.

How far, then, should teachers specialise? There are, indeed, diverse trends apparent here in Member countries. The CERI report on teacher training affirms, for instance, that:

"[An] idea about improving quality in education that is gaining some acceptance is to specialise the trainee teacher more intensively in a particular level of education as a way of targeting the course more effectively and adding depth. This proposal has recently been receiving a good deal of attention in England and Wales" (p. 10)[44].

The recent 1988 Swedish reforms of teacher education, in contrast, have as their explicit purpose the realignment of teacher education to reflect the degree to which the compulsory school years there are seen as a coherent whole rather than sharply divided by the age of the students. The aim is more profound than even establishing coherence between the school system and teacher education as the Swedish report explains:

"... the majority are stressing that the teacher has not only a knowledge-transmitting role but also a socialising one. To safeguard this, Parliament has decided that teachers should have training in more subjects in order to follow their pupils over many grades"[48].

There is, in fact, a wide range of country practice regarding the degree of specialisation in teacher education in terms of the requirements for preparation in specific subject matter – whether, for example, in one, two, or more disciplines. Apart from the educational arguments that may be deployed in favour of greater or lesser concentration on a single discipline, one obvious additional consequence of greater specialisation, particularly insofar as this refers to the age/grade of the pupils to be taught, is a potential corresponding reduction of the margin this leaves for staff redeployment and mobility across the different levels of the system in the face, for example, of swings in enrolments. But that margin may not be a broad one in any event; there is perhaps rather less enthusiasm than hitherto for the proposition of significantly redeploying teachers, across school levels and across subjects, in response to the ebbs and flows of student enrolments. Of course, there will always be some room for using substantial periods of INSET for teacher retraining and reassignment. But to assume that most teachers, given necessary courses, are equally fitted for all types of teaching is to under-estimate seriously the professional knowledge and special understanding applied in different kinds of posts. This is no less true of the expert primary school teacher, possessing the creative ability to convey the whole gamut of the curriculum, establishing a good basis of learning, and understanding child development, as it is of the more commonly cited case of the specialist secondary school subject teacher.

TEACHER ASSESSMENT

Some implications of the research reviewed

This field, perhaps above all the others covered in this report, is one where it is vital for the wisdom and insight of practitioners to mediate the putatively hard evidence of the test or the research. The object of that assessment is the teacher at the fulcrum of the unique combination of pressures ranging from the particular requirements of the subject/level and the overarching (often changing) priorities of national policies, to the particular needs and problems of the local school and community, where each teacher's contribution is as an individual replete with certain knowledge, skills, and capabilities and as a member of a team whose success is to be judged collectively. And today, the whole matter of assessment touches at the heart of the professional identity of the teaching force, involving sometimes the harsh play of politics and ideologies. In the midst of such pressures, it would be foolhardy to expect a body of research to provide simple recipes for action.

An irony of the research is that the very body of literature – on teacher characteristics – which could discover few consistent relationships between those characteristics and student outcomes and has thereby helped to fuel the demand for more formal assessment is, by the same token, unable to point to what that assessment should comprise. In the absence of agreement on what constitutes "competence", "talent", or "incompetence", two primary methods for determining the quality of beginning teachers are widely advocated in the United States. The first is paper and pencil testing on the basis of pre-established criterion scores with the aim of controlling the level of knowledge of teachers coming into the profession. The second is to regulate the nature, content matter, and quality of training of the novice teacher. Problems exist with both. Criterion scores are routinely adjusted to match flows to the supply of and demand for teachers, and while states have been able to alter the course requirements for beginning teachers, the effect on upgrading the quality of teacher education is not always clear. More importantly with respect to the testing, there has been neither a coherent logic or theory on which to structure the assessment instruments nor have the instruments been shown to predict the future quality of the students' teaching. Thus, with the exception of a modest and inconsistent relationship between verbal scores of teachers and student achievement, there is little direct empirical evidence to support these testing policies.

The two methods referred to above, whatever possible doubts about their reliability and validity, more obviously apply to the screening of new entrants than to the assessment of practising teachers unless there is good reason to suspect that the knowledge assessed by the paper and pencil test actually suffers a deterioration in the course of the teacher's career. Does the research reviewed suggest how assessment methods should be designed for those teachers already in the classroom? In fact, a prevalent method with advocates in the United States has been through "research-based" observation instruments in line with the process-product research reviewed earlier. Over the past few years, a sizeable number of states and school districts in the United States have mandated teacher competency assessments using these methods, often as a condition of licensure[49].

Valuable though this work is, there are very real limits to the direct applicability of the process-product line of enquiry – promising indications of good practice are not the same as uniform rules for teaching. First, the components identified as effective in this work are based on correlations of limited general relevance; at best such components apply to teaching in the early school years in well-structured content in reading and mathematics. Second, alternative approaches may be equally effective. Not only might two teachers with contrasting styles teach equally well, but the good teacher will be constantly adapting technique and methods to students and circumstance. Third, the observational approaches display low reliability and lower validity in the terms in which they were constructed, namely to improve student achievement outcomes. On this point, Smith and O'Day conclude:

> "In short, for methodological and theoretical reasons, approaches to the evaluation of teacher competency should *not* be based on presently-existing process-product research" [40].

Those reviewers regard the new work summarised under the label of teacher competency research as potentially valuable. They see it opening up many possible approaches, one of which, in line with the teacher competency methodology, is to observe novice and expert teachers in standardized settings designed to elicit use of their repertoire of relevant knowledge and skills[50]. Although the exact nature of the assessment procedures that this might lead to remains to be worked out, they suggest possible guidelines. First, the teacher performance research establishes a case for assessing the quality and amount of content and pedagogical knowledge of prospective or practicing teachers. Second, the research on teacher thinking provides support for the assessment of a teacher's knowledge of professional practice and the role of being a teacher. Third, there is the beginnings of a methodology for establishing standards of practice based on the observations of expert compared with novice teachers. Progressing from such generalisations to concrete assessment instruments, however, remains a large step. And, no less important, who will be subject to the assessment? By whom? For what reason? When? These critical practical questions of implementation are matters that research cannot resolve.

Considerations for policies

It is a corollary of the diversity of the components that contribute to professionalism and of the teaching force itself (Chapter 3), as well as of the complexity and variability of the ingredients of teaching, as discussed in this chapter, that the "comprehensive" assessment of any teacher's work is a hazardous undertaking. And if the research reviewed above provides few firm guidelines on how such assessment should be conducted, the difficulties are underscored further when the full array of teaching objectives – cognitive and affective development of all students, the special nurturing of target groups of pupils, socialisation, evaluation, the active support of the school as an institution, and so forth – enter the equation. Set against the demand that there should be appraisal of the individual teacher's work in a way that permits ready comparison with others and that is visible, objective, and fair, the order is indeed a tall one.

A great deal hinges on the questions of what the assessment is of, who conducts it, how it will afterwards be deployed, and, not least, whether it is to be the *sole* basis for any decisions concerning staff. A keyword in the foregoing paragraph is "comprehensive" – the search for definitive summary evaluations of teaching competence is a quite different undertaking from the myriad evaluations and assessments undertaken daily in the normal routine of educational practice. It is perhaps worthwhile, therefore, to distinguish "assessment" and "appraisal" where the former refers to any one of a diversity of evaluations of the teacher's tasks, work, and performance using a variety of criteria, while "appraisal" denotes the inclusive judgement of a teacher's qualities overall, though both terms are variously used to denote a variety of practices in different settings and countries.

One consideration that tends to be neglected in the sometimes heated controversies in this field is the degree to which assessment and even appraisal are already a normal feature of educational life. This applies whether the judgement in question concerns prospective teachers in terms of their suitability, the recent entrant and his or her initial performance, the management of a subject department or school, or the selection of staff for promotion. The assessments are different in each case. Some may be purely internal to the institution whereas others may call upon external assessors for inspections of probationary teachers or as members of selection panels for a new school principal or deputy. But in all these cases, judgements and evaluations must be applied. Indeed, there is evidence of a growing perception that many such occasions of existing teacher assessment should be more thoroughly, even professionally, undertaken, precisely in order to ensure fairness for the staff members involved and to protect the educational interests of the pupils and students[51].

These examples serve both to refute the argument that teaching is simply too complex to be assessed and to suggest caution concerning simplistic calls for frequent summary appraisals of all staff. These calls also tend seriously to underestimate the costs involved. Full and regular appraisals that include meaningful classroom observation, assessment of teacher knowledge, the active involvement of senior colleagues and the teacher in question, and the thorough discussion of the implications of the appraisal, whether for professional development or for promotion, will be a costly business in terms of time and financial resources. Still more is this true if the result of the appraisal is the decision for the staff member to undertake in-service training which brings with it its own costs. Thorough-going teacher appraisal system-wide is likely to prove an expensive undertaking.

One type of appraisal that attracts wide publicity is the variety of minimum competency schemes enacted in the 1980s in a number of administrations in the United States to test for basic levels of literacy and numeracy among teachers and even educational administrators. The detractors have maintained, *inter alia*, that the tests are not a reflection of the range of knowledge and skills required in teaching, and the reply has been that the standards required are set at such a basic level, and the pass rate intended to be sufficiently high, that few could object to such a minimal requirement of the teachers of children. If that is the case, and the assessment not simply norm-referenced to fail automatically a fixed proportion, both points of view are hard to fault. It is true that such tests of minimal competency are not, strictly speaking, appraisals of teachers' work at all. But neither can it be seriously maintained that respected professionals do not need to meet basic standards of numeracy and literacy. Indeed the cause for concern might more legitimately be, in this case, that such assessment is needed at all since methods of initial selection were sufficiently remiss to allow those who repeatedly fail the tests to have taken up their posts in the first place[52].

At least three dimensions of assessment and appraisal are raised by this example: the *nature* of the appraisal and the suitability of paper-and-pencil tests; the *object* of the appraisal (all teachers? the very weak? the excellent?); the *result* of the appraisal (staff development? hiring, firing, and promotion?). Cross-cutting these dimensions is the degree to which external assessors/inspectors or teachers are involved in the establishment of criteria and the process of appraisal itself.

Whether appraisal of practising teachers can be conducted without a proper reflection of actual teaching skills and abilities, as opposed to background knowledge, is certainly questionable. As expressed by Bolton: "teacher appraisal without an assessment of performance in the class or lecture room based on direct observation ... is likely to be a fairly broken-backed affair."[53] Not surprisingly, there are misgivings expressed in the United States about use of the National Teacher Examination (NTE) – a paper-and-pencil, multiple choice test – as a valid and reliable indicator of suitability for future teaching even when used as an initial screening device of new entrants. Other paper-and-pencil tests at the state level suffer similar limitations[54]. The problems are magnified if they are intended for the assessment of practising teachers. Indeed, the Educational Testing Service (ETS) that develops the NTE does not even allow states to use it as an assessment instrument for the latter if there are decisions about the conditions of employment that would be based on the scores. Most recently, the NTE has been revised and its use is being coordinated with the National Board for Professional Teaching Standards. The NTE will assess teachers at three different times with the aim of establishing minimum competence for state licensure while the National Board will evaluate teachers after several years' experience on a voluntary basis. It is too early to assess how far these changes have met the worries of the critics.

How far assessments will be school-based or else involve outside appraisal by such bodies as inspectorates will depend very substantially on the traditions of the country in question. Certain OECD countries, notably in the Scandinavian region, report substantial resistance to the notion that schools and teachers should be open to outside inspection, though certain of the same functions of scrutiny and accountability may be fulfilled by the active participation of parents and the community in the running of individual schools. In other cases – such as Belgium, France, Ireland, Italy, the Netherlands, New Zealand, and the United Kingdom – the inspectorate is an established, though not necessarily uncontroversial, feature of the system. Regarding teachers *per se*, a common inspectorate task is to assess suitability for full status at the end of a probationary period.

For practising teachers, the inspectorate role may be still more far-reaching with implications for the future career and promotion prospects of the personnel involved. In France, for example, the inspectorate give individual teachers a periodic ranking on their "pedagogical" accomplishments, alongside the assessment of the administrative fulfilment of duties undertaken by the school. These determine whether the teacher follows one of three trajectories through the salary scale – rapid, medium, slow – and ultimately can affect further promotion prospects once the maximum is attained. Up to now in New Zealand, the teacher can request an inspector's assessment once a certain number of years' experience are gained at a particular level which is then presented as part of the application for promotion[55]. The common assertion that appraisal should have professional development, not rewards, as its exclusive aim tends to ignore the degree to which promotion already is, and should be, decided on merit, implying in turn some form of assessment. The issue comes back instead to how this is undertaken and how far the criteria of validity and equity are fulfilled.

The question of *who* should be the object of appraisal is, if anything, more controversial still. Insofar as the focus is on the school or college, the answer is simple: it should involve all teachers. Nuttall[56] suggests that the qualities necessary for successful teacher appraisal are very similar to those advocated for institutional self-evaluation: one of the prerequisites is a tradition of constructive self-criticism; a climate of trust between teachers and the principal is also essential, together with a commitment to the appraisal processes and an agreement to act on the results. Teachers being appraised should also be involved in the development of the scheme rather than have it imposed upon them, and a good scheme will give teachers some degree of autonomy. Seen in this light, individual teacher and institutional appraisal are two sides of the same process of critical but positive evaluation and review. While such institutionally-based assessment will have the individual's responsibilities and needs well in view, a collective focus on teaching teams, subject departments, and the school as a whole is also relevant.

Once the process of appraisal extends beyond these general characteristics of professionalism to target on particular groups of teachers, however, the requirements of objectivity and equity become immediately pressing, especially if the results of the appraisal will inform decisions on employment status or promotions. With the large majority of class teachers being women and those in leadership roles being men, for example, great care must be taken to ensure that discriminatory judgements are avoided. The issues here also clearly relate closely to those discussed in the previous chapter. The legal status and tenure of teachers powerfully influence the potential of mechanisms for appraisal either in place or proposed. Where teachers are public servants with guaranteed tenure as in many European countries, for instance, radical new forms of appraisal may well sit uneasily with established practice. On the other hand, where these conditions are undergoing revision – for example, where tenure is no longer assured (as in the Netherlands and Sweden) or relicensing is mandatory (as in certain states of the United States) – certain procedures of assessing the teacher's ability to meet at least minimal standards may be an integral component of the change. Moreover, any schemes that seek to enhance the attractiveness of the profession through incentive posts such as "master" or "expert" teacher assume established criteria and processes whereby these posts are allocated. These can be, of course, matters of considerable controversy.

One area that most can agree on in principle, but which presents numerous stumbling blocks in practice, is that the interests of no one are served by the continued service of the patently very weak teacher. Most countries have mechanisms for dismissal in extreme cases but these often apply only to those convicted of criminal or moral misdemeanour. For the purpose of maintaining the morale of competent teachers as well as for protecting the rights of young people to a reasonable education, there should be mechanisms whereby those who are clearly failing their students and colleagues, when reasonable effort at retraining or reallocation have failed, be reassigned out of the classroom or even out of education. These teachers are, in Bolton's words:

"...the utterly hopeless, always a small minority of the teaching force, [who] are a kind of full-stop to any and all worthwhile developments in education. They should never have become teachers, have no feel for, or affinity with, it, and cannot be improved much at all" (p. 2)[53].

90

The issue here may well be the development of satisfactory bureaucratic procedures for retraining and ultimately dismissal that are acceptable to the profession as a whole, rather than the matter of identification. That procedure would need to remain a matter of last resort and avoid casting a pall over the large majority of practising teachers who are competent and reasonably conscientious.

Apart from this small group of very poor teachers, it is impossible to suggest in the abstract how appraisal should be focused. Where professional and staff development, and through that educational improvement, is the main purpose, the focus should perhaps concentrate on the large majority of teachers who do not lie at either end of the spectrum of the "excellent" through to "very poor" (that terminology is to make the brave assumption that those who fall into these two polar categories can be readily identified and recognised). Where, however, the aim is to identify potential principals or candidates for promotion, or else to assess the teachers with special qualities for additional recognition or even reward, the focus is necessarily different. And even for the clearly excellent, appraisal with a view to further professional development does not cease to be relevant; further in-service training may be needed to deepen a specialism, to open up new areas in preparation for additional duties, or simply as reward in itself.

Many of these questions are on current policy agendas across the OECD region. In some countries, certain forms of teacher assessment and appraisal are long-established practice. In others, as in the United States, there are relatively new schemes put in place, and still more recent revisions to them. The United Kingdom is developing a nation-wide system based on extensive trial experimentation though, at the time of writing, its final form remains undecided. The Standing Conference of European Ministers of Education, meeting in Helsinki in May 1987 to discuss "New Challenges for Teachers and their Education", included appraisal as a priority area in its resolution and encouraged further research and exchange between European countries on this theme[57]. Professional solutions are being sought in this field to replace purely ideological debate. Controversy remains, of course, but the principle is increasingly accepted as is recognition of the complexities of the task and the need always for educational objectives to be respected. Ultimately, teacher assessment that meets these criteria may well reinforce, rather than undermine, teacher professionalism.

*

* *

This chapter has considered aspects of the teaching process and the mechanisms and policies for its improvement. It has focused on those aspects that tend to be general to classrooms everywhere, though the specific results of the research surveyed are strictly applicable only to the North American settings that generated these findings. To consider fully the role and function of teachers today, as well as the implications of these for teacher preparation and assessment, requires extending the focus beyond such generalities of good practice to the concrete tasks and challenges that they are faced with in modern societies. To do so draws attention to how demanding are the public and professional expectations on the contemporary teacher. That fact must be kept to the fore in the design of the policy areas discussed in this chapter – teacher education and appraisal. Whether preparation or appraisal is at stake, full account should be taken of the actual circumstances under which teachers practice on the basis of *professionally demanding but attainable* goals. They cannot realistically adopt the standard of the superhuman teacher that few in practice can hope to reach, or, just as importantly, maintain.

NOTES AND REFERENCES

1. Smith, M.S. and O'Day, J. (1988), "Research into Teaching Quality: Main Findings and Lessons for Appraisal" (OECD working document).

2. Mood, A. (ed.) (1970), *Do Teachers Make a Difference?*, United States Office of Education, U.S. Government Printing Office, Washington, DC; Good, Thomas, L., Biddle, Bruce, J. and Brophy, Jere (1975), *Teachers Make a Difference*, Holt, Rinehart and Winston, New York.

3. Coleman, J.S. *et al.* (1966), *Equality of Educational Opportunity*, United States Government Printing Office, Washington, DC. The first IEA survey was in the area of mathematics in 1964 and the results were published in 1967. A number of other IEA surveys were carried out in the late 1960s and early 1970s: for the United States, see Wolf, R.M. (1977), *Achievement in America: National Report of the United States for the International Educational Achievement Project*, Teachers College Press, New York. See also McKnight, C.C. *et al.* (1987), *The Underachieving Curriculum: Assessing U.S. School Mathematics from an International Perspective*, Stripes Publishing Company, Champaign, Illinois.

4. The main earlier works included Mosteller, F. and Moynihan, P. (eds.) (1972), *On Equality of Educational Opportunity*, Random House, New York; Jencks, C. *et al.* (1972), *Inequality: A Reassessment of the Effect of Family and Schooling in America*, Basic Books, New York. Jencks *et al.* used the Equality of Educational Opportunity Survey (EEOS) data but also made extensive use of other data bases. Other reports were also based on the EEOS data including Bowles, S. and Levin, H. (1968), "The Determinants of Scholastic Achievement – An Appraisal of Some Recent Evidence", *Journal of Human Resources*, Vol. 3, No. 1, pp. 3-24; and Hanushek, E.A. and Kain, J.F., "On the Value of 'Equality of Educational Opportunity' as a Guide to Public Policy", in Mosteller, F. and Moynihan, P., *op. cit.* Later works in this category might include Murnane, R.J. (1975), *Impact of School Resources on the Learning of Inner City Children*, Bollinger, Cambridge, MA; Armor, D. *et al.* (1976), *Analysis of the School Preferred Reading Program in Selected Los Angeles Minority Schools*, R 2007-LAUSD, Rand Corporation, Santa Monica, CA; Murnane, R. and Phillips, B. (1981), "What Do Effective Teachers of Inner-City Children Have in Common?" *Social Science Resource*, Vol. 10, No. 1, March, pp. 83-100; Coleman, J., Hoffer, T. and Kilgore, S. (1982), *High School Achievement: Public, Catholic, and Private Schools Compared*, Basic Books, New York; McKnight, C.C. *et al.* (1987), *op. cit.* For a good overview of this class of studies see Hanushek, E.A. (1986), "The Economics of Schooling: Production and Efficiency in Public Schools", *Journal of Economic Literature*, Vol. XXIV, pp. 1141-1177.

5. Four basic methodological problems exist with these data. First, lack of understanding of the process of schooling makes it impossible to know if, or ever, the model of schooling has been adequately specified and, therefore, if effects estimates are accurate. Second, how to measure many of the constructs, such as teacher and curriculum quality and student motivation, that theories of schooling suggest are important? Many researchers with considerable experience of schools are convinced that there is no possibility of ever adequately measuring many of the constructs with survey data. Third, there are serious shortcomings of applying existing standardized achievement scores as appropriate and sensitive measures of student achievement outcomes. Fourth, the studies estimate the effects of existing differences among teachers and schools and

students. If major changes are introduced in the system of schooling, then the estimates of effects would in all likelihood be very different.

6. See Hanushek, E.A. (1986), *op. cit.*

7. The fact that most of the variation in achievement test scores lies within rather than among schools means that existing differences among schools in school-wide characteristics such as average teacher experience or type of teacher training cannot explain much of the variation in individual student achievement scores; they can only explain that part of student achievement that is associated with between-school differences. Similarly, differences within schools can only explain that part of the variation that lies within schools. Typically, when the total variation in student achievement (as measured by standardized achievement tests) is partitioned among and within schools, between 10 and 20 per cent lies among schools. When socio-economic status and other home background characteristics of the student body are controlled for, there is considerably less of the total variation among schools and when prior achievement is also taken into account, the percentage of variation among schools in student achievement scores is even less. After controlling for average home background, the average among-school variance is of the order of 2-3 per cent of the total variation. See Smith, M.S. (1972), "On Equality of Educational Opportunity", in Mosteller, F. and Moynihan, P. (eds.) *op. cit.*; and Jencks, C. *et al.* (1972), *op. cit.*

8. Hanushek, E.A. (1986), *op. cit.*, p. 1164. As Hanushek also points out there is no evidence that the tests used to assess teachers' skills and knowledge for credentialling purposes predict future teaching quality. These tests, such as the National Teacher Examination, typically have a strong verbal component.

9. See Coleman, J., Hoffer, T. and Kilgore, S. (1982), *op. cit.*, and Coleman, J. and Hoffer, T. (1987), *Public and Private High Schools: The Impact of Communities*, New York, Basic Books; see also Purkey, S.C., Stewart, C. and Smith, M.S. (1983), "Effective Schools: A Review", *The Elementary School Journal*, Vol. 83, No. 4, March, pp. 427-452.

10. Hanushek, E.A. (1986), *op. cit.*, pp. 1159-1163. He concludes on the basis of the evidence of five studies, indicating significant variation among teachers, that "teachers and schools differ dramatically in their effectiveness". This is probably an overstatement with respect to schools unless the most effective teachers are systematically assigned to the same schools. However, even if there are only very small differences among the achievement levels of schools on the average, there may be large differences between schools at opposite ends of an effectiveness continuum.

11. Hanushek, E.A. (1986), *op. cit.*

12. See Brophy, J. and Good, T.L. (1986), "Teacher Behavior and Student Achievement", in Wittrock, M. (ed.), *Handbook of Research on Teaching*, 3rd edition, Macmillan, New York, p. 340. Stability coefficients across years ranged from 0.20 to 0.40 in the three studies summarised in that chapter. Though these correlations are relatively small they are certainly not insignificant and indicate that there may be regularly "effective" and "ineffective" teachers.

13. For a comprehensive summary, see Brophy J. and Good. T.L. (1986), *ibid.*

14. The degree of teacher *versus* student control of classroom activity shows a curvilinear (inverted U) relationship to student achievement. Up to a certain point, greater teacher control results in higher achievement; beyond that point, it declines. Brophy, J. and Good, T.L. (1986), *ibid*, p. 337.

15. Barak Rosenshine (1986), "Teaching Functions", in Wittrock, M. (ed.), *op. cit.*

16. Brophy, J. and Good, T.L. (1986), *op. cit.* Many teachers move naturally to this kind of active and interactive approach to teaching. But contrast that with many other teachers whose primary instructional methods are passive while students sit at their desks completing workbooks and worksheets. These teachers initiate and provide little by way of interaction, direct instruction, feedback, and positive or negative effect. With highly-motivated, relatively docile students, the cost of such teachers is "only" in student creativity; with the less well organised and motivated, the loss is of both creativity and fundamental learning.

17. Skinner's machines, for example, have been superseded by many new generations of technology. And the IGE programme, which attempted to build a systematic approach to school-based instruction including student individualisation, in-service teacher training, and building-based research, became too complex to implement well. For a salutory account, see Romberg, T. (ed.) (1985), *Toward Effective Instruction: The IGE Experience*, University Press of America, Lanham, MD.

18. The original mastery learning programme was developed by Benjamin Bloom in the late 1960s based on Carroll's model of school learning. For a more complete discussion of Bloom's ideas, see Bloom, B. (1968), "Learning for Mastery", *Evaluation Comment*, 1. UCLA Center for the Study of Evaluation, Occasional Report No. 9; or Bloom, B. (1976), *Human Characteristics and School Learning*, McGraw-Hill, New York. For reviews of mastery learning research, see Block, J.H. and Burns, R.B. (1976), "Mastery Learning", in Shulman, L.S. (ed.) *Review of Research in Education*, Vol. 4, pp. 3-49, Itasca, Il; Peacock, F.E. and Slavin, R.E. (1987), "Mastery Learning Reconsidered", *Review of Educational Research*, Vol. 57, No. 2, pp. 175-213.

19. Bloom also emphasizes the importance of cues, feedback, participation, and reinforcement, all of which are included in Rosenshine's construct of direct instruction. For a discussion of the relationship between mastery learning and direct instruction, see Hawley, W. *et al.* (1984), "Good Schools: What Research Says about Improving Student Achievement", *Peabody Journal of Education*, Vol. 61, No. 4, pp. 43-45.

20. Bloom claims an effective size of nearly 1.0 standard deviation, and two recent meta-analyses found effects almost as large, ranging from 0.52 to 0.94 of a standard deviation for different groups of students. See Bloom, B.S. (1984), "The 2 Sigma Problem: The Search for Methods of Instruction as Effective as One-to-One Tutoring", *Educational Researcher*, Vol. 13, pp. 4-16; Guskey, T.R. and Gates, S.L. (1985), "A Synthesis of Research on Group-Based Mastery Learning Programs", paper presented at the annual meeting of the American Educational Research Association, Chicago; Kulik, C.L., Kulik, J.A. and Bangert-Drowns, R.L. (1986), "Effects of Testing for Mastery on Student Learning", paper presented at the annual meeting of the American Educational Research Association, San Francisco. For a detailed discussion of the shortcomings of the research and a less glowing assessment, see Slavin, R.E. (1987), "Mastery Learning Reconsidered", *Review of Educational Research*, Vol. 57, No. 2. A similarly modest conclusion is reached by Stallings, J. and Stipek, D. (1986), "Research on Early Childhood and Elementary School Teaching Programs", in Wittrock (ed.), *op. cit.* in note 12, pp. 742-746.

21. In group-based mastery learning programmes, the amount of time required for most students to attain mastery is also a critical consideration. If the additional time is provided outside regular classroom instruction, then the programme becomes expensive and difficult to implement. If the additional time is provided during regular hours of instruction, then higher achievers must wait for lower achieving students to catch up. This may lead to what some researchers have called a "Robin Hood effect" in which low achievers benefit at the expense of their more highly achieving peers. See Slavin, R.E. (1987), *op. cit.* for a discussion of this problem.

22. Olson, L. (1985), "Chicago Scuttles Mastery Learning Reading Plan After $7.5 Million, 5-Year Commitment", *Education Week*, August 21. Critics charged that the CMLR programme, which continues to be used in hundreds of United States school districts, dampens children's enthusiasm and ability to read by presenting reading as a set of fragmented tasks. In addition, they argued that the materials contained grammatical errors, illogical constructions, disjointed units, and reading passages that were too short to develop comprehension skills.

23. Cohen, P.A., Kulik, J.A. and Kulik, C.L. (1982), "Educational Outcomes of Tutoring: A Meta-Analysis", *American Educational Research Journal*, Vol. 19, pp. 237-248.

24. See Greenwood, C.R., Whorton, D. and Delquadri, J.C. (1984), "Tutoring Methods", *Direct Instruction News*, Vol. 3, No. 3, pp. 4-7, 23.

25. Stallings, J. and Stipek, D. (1986), *op. cit.* See also Cohen, E. (1986), *Designing Groupwork: Strategies for Heterogeneous Classrooms*, Teachers College Press, New York.

26. See also Slavin R.E. (1980), "Cooperative Learning", *Review of Educational Research*, Vol. 50, pp. 317-343.

27. Corno, L. and Snow, R.E. (1986), "Adapting Teaching to Individual Differences Among Learners", in Wittrock (ed.) *op. cit.* in note 12. This chapter contains a detailed and sophisticated review of ATI research.

28. Peterson, P. (1986), "Selecting Students and Services for Compensatory Education: Lessons from Aptitude-Treatment Interaction Research", paper delivered at the Conference on the Effects of Alternate Designs in Compensatory Education, Washington, DC, June.

29. See, for example, Ogbu, J. and Matute-Bianchi, M.E. (1986), "Understanding Sociocultural Factors: Knowledge, Identity, and School Adjustment", in *Beyond Language: Social and Cultural Factors in Schooling Language Minority Students*, Evaluation, Dissemination, and Assessment Center; California State University, L.A. For a discussion of this issue in relation to bilingual education, language acquisition, and school success, see Cummins, J. (1986), "Empowering Minority Students: A Framework for Intervention", *Harvard Educational Review*, Vol. 56, No. 1. Cummins asserts that "minority students are disabled or disempowered by schools in very much the same way that their communities are disempowered by interactions with societal institutions" p. 23). Incorporation of the students' language and culture into the school programme, he argues, becomes a means of "empowering" those students and thus fostering their academic success. For a discussion of these issues in relation to linguistic minority students in European countries, see Skutnab-Kangas, T. (1984), *Bilingualism or Not: The Education of Minorities*, Multilingual Matters, Cleveland (United Kingdom).

30. For a discussion of the shortcomings of this research, see Shulman, L.S. (1986), "Paradigms and Research Programs in the Study of Teaching: A Contemporary Perspective", in Wittrock (ed.) *op. cit.* in note 12.

31. Tharpe, R. (1988), "4V + 2K = A Formula for Minority Student Success". Presentation at the first Stanford Centennial Conference on educating children at risk, School of Education, Stanford University, February 26.

32. This point is emphasized in Peterson's discussion *op. cit.* of ATI research and teacher effectiveness and in much of the process-product work on active teaching.

33. Brophy, J. (1986), "Research Linking Teacher Behavior to Student Achievement: Potential Implications for Instruction of Chapter I Students". Paper delivered at the Conference on Effects of Alternate Designs in Compensatory Education, Washington DC, June.

34. Peterson, P. (1986), *op. cit.* See also Corno, L. and Snow, R.E. (1986), *op. cit.*

35. Shulman, L.S. (1986), *op. cit.*; and Shulman, L.S. (1987), "Knowledge and Teaching: Foundations of the New Reform", in *Harvard Educational Review*, Vol. 57, No. 1. Much of the material in this section is based on these papers.

36. For reviews of this work, see Resnick, L. B. (1987), *Education and Learning to Think*, National Academy Press, Washington DC, p. 45; and Glaser, R. (1984), "Education and Thinking: The Role of Knowledge", *American Psychologist*, Vol. 39, February, pp. 93-104.

37. Jackson, P.W. (1968), *Life in Classrooms*, Holt, Reinhart and Winston, New York.

38. Clark, C.M. and Peterson, P.L. (1986), "Teachers' Thought Processes", in Wittrock (ed.), *op. cit.* in note 12.

39. For a discussion of this work see Shulman, L.S. (1986), "Those Who Understand: Knowledge Growth in Teaching", *Educational Researcher*, February, pp. 4-14.

40. Addendum to Smith, M.S. and O'Day, J. (1988), *op. cit.* communicated to the Secretariat.

41. Discussed in Bradley, H.W. (1987), "Quality of Education and Development in Teacher Training: A Case Study of England and Wales" (OECD working document).

42. See the discussion in Darling-Hammond, L. and Berry, B. (1988), *The Evolution of Teacher Policy*, The Rand Corporation, JRE-01, Santa Monica, CA.

43. Neave, G. (1987), "Challenges Met: Trends in Teacher Education, 1975-1985", *Introduction to New Challenges for Teachers and their Education: National Reports on Teacher Education*. Standing Conference of European Ministers of Education, Council of Europe, Strasbourg.

44. OECD/CERI(1988), "New Trends in Teacher Training: A Preliminary View". (OECD working document prepared for the International Conference on Teacher Training for Basic Education held in Novi-Sad, Yugoslavia, 3-5 October 1988).

45. Könnölä, J. and Merilainen, K. (1988), "Teachers in Finland" (OECD working document) p. 24; and Spyropoulos, G.P. (1988), "La formation des enseignants en Grèce" (OECD working document, French text only), p. 35.

46. Jeuthe, E. (1989), "Teachers in Germany: The Employment of Teachers against the Background of Teacher Surplus, the Ageing of the Profession, and a Decline of Student Numbers" (OECD working document), p. 2.

47. Discussed in detail in OECD (1989), *Pathways for Learning: Education and Training from 16 to 19*, Paris.

48. Andrén, B., Lovgren, E. and Skog-Ostlin, K. (1987), "Teachers in Sweden" (OECD working document), p. 1.

49. Sandufer, J.T. (1986), "State Assessment Trends", *AACTE Briefs*, Vol. 7, No. 6, pp. 12-14. McLaughlin, M.W. and Pfeifer, R.S. (1986), *Teacher Evaluation: Learning for Improvement and Accountability* (Report No. 86-SEPI-5), Stanford Education Policy Institute, Stanford, CA.

50. See Shulman, L.S. (1987), *op. cit.* in note 35.

51. See, for example, Wilson, J.D., Thomson, G.O.B., Millward, B. and Keenan, T. (1989), *Assessment for Teacher Development* (Proceedings of an International Seminar, Edinburgh, Scotland, June 1987), Falmer Press, London; and Morgan, C., Hall, V. and MacKay, H. (1983), *The Selection of Secondary Headteachers*, Open University Press, Milton Keynes.

52. One of the most publicised recent examples of testing practising teachers occurred in Texas in 1985 when all teachers in that state were given a "basic skills minimum competency test". Based on previously established cut-off points, a substantial number of teachers (but a low percentage) "failed" and were put on probation until they had retaken the test and passed. A second number of teachers declined to do this and retired from teaching. The advocates of the policy argue that they got rid of incompetent teachers. The opponents pointed to the lack of validity of the test and the cost. See Shepard, L. and Kreitzer, A. (1987), "The Texas Teacher Test", *Educational Researcher*, Vol. 16, No. 6, pp. 22-31 for a history and critical view of this episode.

53. Bolton, E.J. (1988), "The Characteristics of Good Teachers and Good Teaching: An Inspectorate Viewpoint" (OECD working document), p. 7.

54. For a discussion of these issues, see Haertel, E. (1987), "Validity of Teacher Licensure and Teacher Education Admissions Tests". Paper prepared for the National Education Association and Council of Chief State School Officers, Stanford University, September.

55. OECD (1988), "Teachers in New Zealand" (OECD working document), pp. 8-9.

56. Nuttall, D. (1986), "What Can We Learn from Research on Teaching and Appraisal?", in *Appraising Appraisal*, British Education Research Association (BERA).

57. Council of Europe (1987), *New Challenges for Teachers and their Education: Report on the fifteenth session of the Strasbourg Conference of European Ministers of Education*, Strasbourg.

Chapter 5

NEW TASKS AND CHALLENGES

AN EXTENDED ROLE FOR THE TEACHER

"The tasks of teachers are today more complex and demanding than in the past. They have to respond to the wishes of parents regarding educational outcomes, the social need for wider access to education, and pressures for more democratic participation within the schools."

OECD Ministers of Education[1]

"The task of teaching has become more difficult today than it was yesterday. What will it be like tomorrow?"

The Lesourne Report to the French
Minister of Education[2]

"The school teacher's task is increasingly complex and demanding".

Introduction to the United Kingdom
White Paper "Teaching Quality"[3]

"In recent years, in many societies, it has quite clearly been the case that more and more responsibilities have been placed upon teachers, and the role of the teacher has become even more complicated and difficult".

Denis Lawton: Rapporteur to the OECD enquiry
on the "Condition of Teaching"[4]

"The more important education becomes, both for society as a whole and the individual subject, the more demands are made on education. At the same time as we note a change in the professional status of teachers and tendencies towards the de-qualification of teachers' work, we can also see that the new goals and the new demands on education require a more educated and more professional teacher".

Ulf Lundgren: Report to the Standing
Conference of European Ministers of Education[5]

In theory at least, the consensus is clear: education's responsibilities, and hence those of teachers, have become more extensive and complex than in the past. More is expected from them in contributing towards, or even resolving, a whole array of economic, social, and cultural problems, while perceived shortcomings in these different domains commonly inspire the charge "youngsters failed by schools and teachers". The teacher, as Lundgren alludes to in the passage above, is at once more exposed to criticisms and yet given an ever-expanding brief. It is an open question, therefore, how far that extended role, while officially accorded, has been fully recognised in practice, and whether appropriate changes have been correspondingly implemented in teacher conditions, rewards, and preparation.

To account for these developments is to address the very complexity and interdependence of late 20th century societies[6]. These societies are typified by the growing specialisation of educational functions in that custodial and socialisation responsibilities have been gradually transferred from parents, families, communities, and churches, and entrusted to education systems. Even in simple quantitative terms, an increasing proportion of families are typified by both parents, where there are two living together, going out to work (Table 5 showed clearly how significant has been the growth of female labour force participation). At the same time, many societies are witnessing a marked increase in the numbers of lone-parent families. Estimates for these stand at as many as a quarter of all families with children in the United States and at least one in ten in many other OECD countries[7]. It is to be expected that these secular pressures will continue in the future; the shift from general labour surplus to the emergence of shortages and the continuation of high rates of marital dissolution will no doubt maintain the custodial and socialisation importance of schools, quite apart from their manifest function of imparting knowledge. These pressures also have more immediate educational implications: the demand for pre-school and pre-primary provision grows apace across OECD countries (as it does for post-compulsory education and training) while school systems are being increasingly asked to reorder their schedules to accommodate parental working patterns. All this gives rise to a further anomaly: schools and colleges are expected to perform a leading role in raising the young at a time when, as described in Chapter 1, parents and communities are seeking a greater measure of account-ability and participation for themselves in educational decision-making. More is expected of teachers, that is, just as they come in for greater scrutiny and their freedom of action is subject to the curtailment of outside influence.

Conflicting pressures on teachers are apparent too in terms of sources of knowledge and culture. The pervasive growth of the media has meant that young people have a variety of alternatives from which to draw their inspiration, knowledge, and values, not all of which are compatible with the ethos of schools and the style of classroom learning. Arguably, the written word has been devalued relative to other modes of communication. Attitudes to the adult world and the authority of teachers have no doubt also changed. Yet responsibility for shortcomings in the learning and behaviour of youngsters tend disproportionately to be laid at education's – and, ultimately, the teacher's – door, even though their actual influence has been curtailed or supplemented by these alternatives. Proper societal assessment of the effects of the media on the upbringing and socialisation of the young has scarcely been undertaken, still less its impact on the tasks and responsibilities of teachers.

The social and economic aspirations of the general population continue to grow apace. Whether or not those aspirations are realistic in terms of all gaining access to high levels of socio-economic rewards and privileges, education is commonly accorded a central role for their attainment. The widening responsibilities of education, and concomitantly of the teacher, have both an absolute and a distributional side. Expectations are high and growing while more of the population seek to enjoy the benefits that education is held to bring. Such a broadening and deepening of demands has its equivalent at the level of the individual teacher. What once would have been regarded as exceptional devotion to duty has now become viewed as normal practice.

There is a further dimension of education's exposure to high demands that comes to rest on the shoulders of teachers. The contemporary language of educational policy and media coverage is predominently one of "change", "reform", "improvement". Scarcely has one set of reforms been formulated, let alone properly implemented, and another is in genesis. Yet educational reform is necessarily a long-term process if it is to be genuine and lasting. From the inception of a reform to its dissemination and acceptance takes time. A further significant time lag is then involved for this to be translated into appropriate teacher education, retraining, and the reorganisation of learning resources and a further lag still to actual change of classroom or workshop practice. Education systems are repeatedly typified as the sluggish resistors of new ideas and outside influences, thereby providing additional fuel to the pressure for more reform. While there is undoubtedly an element of conservatism in all systems, the critics give sparse attention to the implications of advocating constant, rapid flux and adaptability in schools, whether in terms of teacher re-education and the reorganisation of learning, or of how established educational objectives would be realised, or of the common resistance among parents and the media to the untried. Implementing real change may depend less on the constant introduction of still more reforms, and instead call for the concentration on priorities.

Having said that, teachers cannot escape from the modern pressures for change and it is right that societies expect the highest levels of competence and commitment from them. But as societies continue to broaden and alter education's brief, a deliberate societal effort may well be called for to arrive at a more focused ambit of educational responsibilities, that would include clarification of what initial education should aim at and what is to be sustained through different forms of lifelong learning. In that reappraisal, a key element should be the establishment of a demanding but realistic specification of what is expected of teachers, recognising that continually adding new duties may well run counter to the search for clearer definitions of teacher tasks and teaching competence.

Such reappraisal touches at the heart of the effort in some countries to establish more clearly-defined contractual duties for teachers. The exercise of determining the content of the teacher's responsibilities in very concrete terms can be expected to influence the exercise of professional duties. Opposing arguments can be made: that more clearly-defined contractual duties limit professionalism by adopting the model – to return to the typology introduced in Chapter 3 – of the "teacher as worker", or they might enhance it through exposure of how extensive those duties have become and/or the concentration on those tasks specifically to do with teaching itself. The question of the proper distribution of tasks between teachers, as the professionals with principal responsibilities for instructional duties, and other personnel is certainly a relevant one here.

Opposing arguments can also be made in terms of whether teacher professionalism is promoted or constrained by the sharing of responsibilities with other specialists, either employed within the schools or from external agencies. On the one hand, a more focused definition of duties on instruction and learning *per se* may act to clarify the nature of teachers' claims to professional recognition in terms of specific pedagogical and subject knowledge and expertise. On the other hand, the creation and growth of separate professional specialisms for treating such problems as learning difficulties or emotional disturbance in the young or for different forms of counselling may arguably result in a narrowing of teacher expertise through setting up a more complex division of labour for the education of the young. Either way, the establishment of more clearly-defined contractual duties must confront the wide-ranging tasks and challenges now involved in raising and educating the young.

SPECIFIC TASKS AND CHALLENGES

The foregoing paragraphs discussed the broadening of the teacher's brief in general terms. This section identifies a number of the specific challenges now confronting teachers in many OECD countries. The selection made can only be indicative of the new measures and aims that comprise contemporary policy and their treatment makes no pretence even to summarise the major issues arising with each. The aim instead is to put concrete flesh on the bones of the general argument and in so doing to underline a common feature of each policy or measure: specific avenues for reform – whether introducing computers into the classroom or mainstreaming disabled pupils or devising new forms of "teacher-intensive" student assessment or implementing gender equality policies or whatever – tend to be designed and promoted with their educational benefits uppermost, and their implications for the total life of schools and teachers only secondarily, if at all. And yet their successful implementation depends ultimately on the knowledge, skills, and enthusiasm of teachers and their collective ability to organise the learning process to incorporate them accordingly.

This is not to say that the question of implementation itself is ignored in reform proposals. But it is to observe that implementation is normally approached through the identification of the conditions necessary to realise the aims of the discrete reforms in terms of the students and learning needs rather than how those aims align in practical terms with all the other demands made on schools, teachers, and teacher training programmes. Thus the advocates of, for example, gender equality or integration of the handicapped or the widespread use of information technologies in schools can forcefully argue how, with its extensive coverage in teacher education and retraining, a school-based review and reorganisation process geared to that strategy, and supporting backup (not to mention radical revisions of teachers' attitudes), their particular set of proposals can become reality. Each strategy taken by itself can thus be viewed as ambitious but ultimately feasible. The uppermost consideration for schools and practising teachers, however, is what *all* the proposals for change add up to for the teacher's task, both in terms of individual performance and collective organisation. No single reform strategy, in other words, can be realistically proposed without due consideration given to how it fits in with all the other reform strategies on current agendas in terms of teacher time, preparedness, and the maximisation of collective effort. That is the comprehensive perspective in which specific reform strategies need to be framed.

Curriculum reform and pupil assessment

Reforms of the curriculum and of student assessment generally call on teachers to have a greater répertoire of skills and more advanced professional attitudes than in the past[8]. Teaching traditional curricula was in many respects a relatively simple matter: to caricature slightly, the teacher possessed a certain amount of knowledge (mostly factual information) which had to be learned and reproduced by the pupils. The teacher's task was to present the information in manageable packages, the pupils memorised the information, and after an interval the teacher tested the pupils' recall. Correct and incorrect answers could easily be identified and pupils given a mark without difficulty.

Reformed curricula and assessment procedures are altogether more challenging – for teachers and pupils. There is less emphasis on memorisation of content and more concern with understanding. In history, for example, it implies less emphasis on dates and narrative and more on understanding relationships between historical forces and life-styles of people living in earlier epochs[9]. For such learning to be effective, the teacher must have a very good grasp of the subject matter, as discussed in the previous chapter, which is partly a question of insight into the "structure" of the discipline or subject, including the ability to identify key concepts, ideas, and generalisations. Teachers must also be able to transmit this more abstract knowledge, again more difficult than the simple presentation of facts to be stored. Some new curricula involve active styles of pupil learning, for example acquiring and practising historical skills rather than the passive learning of secondhand materials. Giving pupils the opportunity to "solve historical problems" by working with documents can present problems of pedagogy and of classroom organisation and control. And teachers may also confront criticism from parents and other members of the public for failing to teach "real" subject matter[10]. Teachers, individually and collectively, are increasingly called upon to be leading agents in curriculum design. With the common trend to replace or supplement examinations with continuous assessment, teachers are also more actively involved in the marking and credentialling process. Other forms of student evaluation, such as profiles that cover a wide range of abilities and achievements and are intended to supply a more complete reflection of a student's merits than the examination mark, are all more demanding of teacher time and input.

Curriculum and examination reform in the United Kingdom provides good illustrative examples of the skills and co-operative abilities of teachers that would have been little called for in the past. With the introduction of a new public examination in England and Wales, the General Certificate of Secondary Education (GCSE), schools are more closely implicated in the detailed design of the curriculum within the broad syllabus and assessment guidelines, and in the assessment of students' work that previously would have been externally examined. One account of the development of "core skills" programmes in Scotland, adopting criterion-referenced methods of assessment and involving the very active co-operation of teachers, employers, and different training agencies in programme design, shows clearly the extended range of skills and responsibilities required of teachers in that case[11].

A CERI review has recently been undertaken of curriculum trends across OECD countries[12]. Generalising across schools and countries is difficult but it is possible to discern, for the primary school cycle in particular, the following four factors as currently exercising a strong influence on the direction of curriculum reforms:

- The pace with which the information technology revolution and the use of computers in schools progress (see below);
- The widespread consensus that broadly-defined cognitive skills should be cultivated across the whole curriculum;
- Growing public awareness of the precariousness of human life on the planet and the need for schooling to foster in children awareness of values, environmental and aesthetic sensitivity, and various other personal/cultural development initiatives;
- The drive towards greater structure and coherence, more rigorous assessments, accountability for outcomes, and more formal procedures in teaching.

The same CERI review adjudged that, overall, significant curriculum reforms have been apparent though still not on a sufficient scale to match the structural economic and social changes of recent decades. Still more might thus be expected of teachers in the future. Reform has been most noticeable at the primary level, typified in many OECD countries by the development of innovative learning strategies, the incorporation of new subject areas (such as computer studies and integrated science and social studies), and greater recourse to problem-centred learning. At the secondary level, the scale of reform has been less marked, though here the review notes that "the most obvious and interesting" changes have occurred in the interface between vocational and general education. This is a matter not only of the formal content of programmes but of the approach of teachers to economic and employment factors that imbues the whole life of the school or college. There is the increasing call for teachers, especially in secondary schools, to be aware of the worlds of employment and work, to impart positive attitudes among their students towards entry into active life, and to give informed guidance as appropriate. This is over and above the formal addition of a greater vocational element to the curriculum itself[13]. That can scarcely be realised without greater contact on a systematic basis between schools and teachers, on the one hand, and employers and the labour market, on the other. The responsibilities here are two-way; the teaching profession needs to be more outward-looking, but so too must the world of work make itself available in an active way towards schools, giving teachers the opportunity to foster that outside contact.

Further examples are relevant here. For instance, "internationalisation" has emerged as a recognised priority. The impending integration within the European Community in 1992, as well as the other political and cultural changes in Europe more broadly defined, are among the most tangible evidence of this but the importance of languages, cultural understanding, and awareness of international affairs is more long-standing and general and applies to all OECD countries. What is especially new, and this is where education comes in, is the widespread recognition that without change in attitudes and linguistic abilities, concomitant with the opening of frontiers and the interdependence of nations, grave economic and political consequences are likely to ensue for any country. Obviously, teachers are key actors in bringing about such change. Other additional responsibilities for schools and teachers are no less contemporary. One is that of enhancing awareness of the environment and pollution and of developing environmental studies as part of the curriculum[14]. Other examples could be added to the list such as attention to sexual and moral issues such as drug abuse or AIDS, or of looking for signs of the physical abuse of children. What is common to these examples is that schools and teachers are called upon to play their part in developing active citizens, not passive consumers or recipients of knowledge. In fact, they imply a much broader conception of "school knowledge" and embrace values and attitudes to citizenry. That is altogether a more challenging brief for teachers than the one they held in times gone by. The same basic question resurfaces: how well prepared are they, individually and collectively, to meet these challenges?

Targeted reform strategies

Three areas of targeted reform, that embrace not only, or even principally, the revision of curricular offerings but pedagogical practices and the organisation of learning within the institution, can be singled out as warranting particular attention: multiculturalism[15], gender equality policies[16], and the integration of disabled pupils into mainstream educational provision[17]. Though the targets are very different in each case, there are parallels that can be drawn between them. One parallel is that each of these policy areas sprang initially from the need to address the educational disadvantages suffered by specific sections of the student population. As programmes developed and measures were tried, however, aims have often come to be set more widely. The approach of "special needs measures", however valuable where remedial help is required, can be seen to be limited and partial since it implies additional efforts rather than full integration within the curriculum. Perspectives have thus enlarged beyond that of "target groups" on the grounds that policies for multiculturalism or gender equality or the integration of the disabled will remain of marginal effectiveness and even miss their target altogether unless all pupils and students are brought in. The new challenges for teachers in these cases are thus twofold: first, the number of strategic considerations and targeted programmes that enter into day-to-day teaching is growing; second, each one of these strategies has come to be defined more ambitiously over the past decade or so. Instead of catering for "special needs" (which could be met with appropriate specialist staff), the perspectives have enlarged to demand full integration in the curriculum, impinging, therefore, on the work of *all* teachers.

While the parallels exist between these selected policy areas, there are, of course, crucial differences between them and each deserves specific examination. Concerning *multiculturalism*, one problem area for schools and teachers in defining a response is the sheer number and variety of cultural, linguistic, and ethnic populations within and between the different OECD countries. How far can the education service strive to meet the specific needs and claims of each one? How equipped are existing teachers to teach flexible multicultural programmes and how well does the current intake of teachers correspond to the present variety of ethnic and cultural groups in society? Though strident demands and assertions are commonplace in this domain, for the most part teachers must cope with realising multicultural education in the absence of commonly agreed ideas of what they are striving towards. There are competing schools of thought that place quite differing emphases on such matters as whether there should be a separate place for multicultural education in the curriculum and what that should be, the importance of linguistic instruction to the multicultural issue, how the host language and culture should be regarded, the relative emphasis placed on combatting educational disadvantage, and the handling of multicultural issues in schools of predominantly majority student intake. However the school and its teachers interpret their duty on these matters, some will be left dissatisfied.

As with the other areas discussed in this chapter, the relevant point is not simply that the curriculum is in the process of being broadened. It is also that the teacher is expected to be an agent in the negotiation and the realisation of more active learning that involves students, parents, and communities – altogether a more difficult undertaking than the traditional transmission of clearly-defined "school knowledge". One author has described the wider perspectives brought to bear on multiculturalism as a move from one of overriding concern with discrimination to the quest for recognition, defined in terms that the ethnic and cultural groups in question are fully party to[18]. This issue affects, of course, practising teachers but it raises sharply too the matter of the recruitment of minority teachers into schools and colleges. Most minorities remain seriously under-represented in the teaching forces of OECD countries.

Gender equality raises its own questions and challenges, as well as uncertainties, for teachers and for school policies more broadly defined. The models passed on by the staff to the students from the patterns of deployment described in Chapter 2 – women teachers predominant in pre-primary and primary education and in the "female" subjects; men in leadership positions and teaching "male" subjects – provide a major stumbling block to change in student choices and attitudes. So, gender equality policies are about teachers in the most direct way, not only their realisation *through* teaching but in the very staffing practices of schools. The alteration of these staffing patterns implies close scrutiny of methods of recruitment and promotion as suggested in Chapter 3 but those patterns also stem from the entrenched differences of educational choices made by females and males throughout education systems that become ultimately reflected in teacher supply. Increasingly, concern about gender equality has focused on the myriad of conscious and unconscious ways that teachers treat boys and girls differently[19]. By its very ingrained nature, teacher behaviour in this regard is very resilient to change. It can be partly addressed in the course of pre-service teacher education, though that alone is hardly sufficient to redress such a deep-seated phenomenon. Proponents of reform have thus come to give much attention to the need for coherent whole-school strategies if gender equality initiatives are not to depend on the individual efforts of committed staff[20]. Of such initiatives, the most widely adopted have been those aimed at eliminating sex stereotypes from textbooks and teaching, removing differences in curricular and timetable opportunities between female and male students, and promoting non-traditional choices and programmes for girls and young women, especially in the sciences and in particular technical and vocational subjects.

There are some parallels to be drawn here with the discussion of multicultural strategies. Schools and teachers face a similar lack of clarity in the operational direction of change and a set of possibly inconsistent public demands. The concrete aims of gender equality in education are open to a variety of interpretations as are the opinions expressed on the matter, often vociferously, by parents and in the community, by no means always in favour of greater equality of treatment between the sexes. Meanwhile, teachers are left to resolve these differences in their everyday practice as they are to cope with possible conflicts between adherence to multicultural understanding and the promotion of gender equality when certain cultural and religious groups are against the promotion of women. And, also in parallel with multiculturalism, the notion of gender equality is coming to be viewed more comprehensively than simply to mean addressing the education and training of girls and women, challenging though this is. It means serious scrutiny of the upbringing and education of males too, which is potentially a more radical and controversial undertaking since it invites questioning of some of the most profound attitudes and values of OECD societies. Far-reaching gender equality in education is likely to be as much about the socialisation and choices of boys as it is of rectifying inequities concerning girls.

The integration of the disabled is another official policy goal shared by many OECD countries. "Integration" may be more or less far-reaching; the more completely that it is accomplished, the more demanding it is likely to be on the organisational skills of the staff and the individual teacher, on their expertise and co-operation, and on support facilities. One classification of stages or "models" of integration, in terms of degrees of implementation, is as follows[21]:

– *The Island Integration Model*: the "special needs" pupils are educated in a self-contained classroom set aside for them in an ordinary school.
– *The Teacher-Deal Model*: integration occurs through informal arrangements, and resources are only offered on an *ad hoc* basis.
– *The Unconditional Integration Model*: in this model, integration involves all aspects of the mainstream school. Integration does not take place in one classroom, or only at intervals, but instead is regarded as a permanent and all-pervasive feature of the school.

For integration to become an accepted and normal feature of educational life, the latter is clearly viewed by proponents as the ideal. Beyond the specific changes of classroom practice, reorganisation at the institutional level is likely to call for school-wide planning, well-organised systematic procedures to involve the parents of special needs students in their children's education, the development of appropriate means of assessing pupil and class progress, as well as adequate support structures and facilities. Each, of course, is demanding on teacher time and expertise.

As with the other strategic areas, the full implications of thorough-going integration are far-reaching for teacher education, both pre-service and, still more, in-service. In-service provision, school-based INSET especially, is a key element of successful implementation. The object of that provision should address as much teacher attitudes as their specialist knowledge of learning difficulties and integration strategies if mainstreaming is to become a reality. One conclusion to emerge from research is the generally negative or hesitant attitudes held by teachers towards the thorough-going integration of the disabled into classes[22]. Another conclusion is that the success of integration cannot depend on the "super-teachers" – the exceptionally dedicated and hard-working individuals committed to making it work – because, by definition, these are out-of-the-ordinary and because they are liable to burn out[21]. Still more does this conclusion apply when integration is placed alongside the other demands on schools and teachers. The challenge for policy design is not simply the acknowledgement of the need for integration to depend on the more normal contribution of staff than can be offered by the exceptionally motivated "super-teacher" but to realise the conditions whereby that contribution becomes part of ordinary school practice.

The challenge of information technologies

A specific new challenge affecting large numbers of teachers is the spread and use of information technologies (ITs) in education. A CERI report prepared earlier in the 1980s categorised the different patterns that countries were then pursuing in introducing ITs in schools as the "vocational" approach (where ITs are introduced primarily as a response to the need for specialised human resources), the "comprehensive" approach (where informatics is regarded as an element of general education for all), the "equipment" approach (priority given to investment in equipment as a variant of the "vocational" approach), and the "curriculum" approach (purely educational concerns are uppermost here, especially curriculum development for ITs)[23]. A more recent survey of the extent to which countries have introduced microcomputers in schools has refined the picture further – there is more equipment in secondary than in primary schools while the patterns of use at the two levels are often different. Microcomputers are deployed at the primary level mainly for teaching traditional subjects and basic skills. In secondary schools in many (but not all) countries, microcomputers have led primarily to the creation of new subjects such as computer awareness at junior levels, and computer science at senior secondary levels and in vocational schools[24].

While the IT advocates enthusiastically look forward to revolutionary changes to teaching and learning, it should be underlined that the actual impact of the new technology is not simple or one-way. It depends very much on the choices made about how it should be used. The range of possible uses is broad. Microcomputers can provide the basis for the introduction of new subjects to the curriculum or for the development of new topics within existing subjects. As teaching tools, they can be used to replicate and perhaps reduce the drudgery of known teaching methods such as drill and practice, or, more radically exploited, to structure learning based on exploration and discovery. They may be integral to new approaches to the assessment and monitoring of student progress. Most radically, they can potentially open up approaches to learning which could not be envisaged in the absence of computer technology[25].

The practicability and success of new approaches depend crucially on the attitudes and capacities of teachers. Far from diminishing the "teacher factor", the use of microcomputers depends on teachers being ready and able to learn new content and methods of classroom management. To the extent that they are used in applications more complex than simple drill and practice, teachers can usefully become directly involved in applied research into what is taught and how it is learned. By extension, this implies that they should become still fuller partners in the development of curriculum and the specification of software. To formalise and disseminate the knowledge that they develop, expert teachers may need to be released from their regular duties to work with development teams. Each of these different elements in the successful development and everyday use of ITs in schools carries, of course, its own implications for teacher preparation, pre- and in-service, the availability of teacher time, and the appropriate organisation of learning. In this connection, new co-ordinating structures may be needed to ensure that teachers are trained in sufficient numbers and on applications in line with the likely educational uses of microcomputers and the probable access to hardware and software within the school. But it is also an awkward reality that this field, perhaps above all others dealt with in this chapter, is subject to very rapid change. An emerging problem is the difficulty for the teacher to choose between the hundreds of available alternative software learning packages, short of viewing and trying each one[26]. This too suggests the potential value of co-ordinated structures to provide information and advice to teachers.

Decentralisation

The enhanced professional role for teachers in such matters as curriculum design and implementation and pupil assessment, as discussed earlier, may be regarded as one specific aspect of the general issue of the decentralisation of educational decision-making and the impact that this has on teachers' roles and responsibilities. It is important to emphasize, however, that the term "decentralisation" can be used to cover many different forms of change, not all of which result in greater decision-making power at the level of the teacher. It may refer to a "regionalisation" of powers previously held by central authorities (as in France and Spain) that may not necessarily alter the teacher's exercise of professional duties. It may refer to the strengthening of local accountability and parental and community involvement which, though often extending the *responsibilities* of teachers (and school leaders in particular), does not necessarily imply a corresponding extension of their *powers*. Nor are all countries moving along the same trajectories towards decentralisation or, where they are, there may be simultaneous centralising tendencies, especially in the areas of curriculum, content and the assessment of performance (Australia, Sweden, and the United Kingdom all exhibit such diametric development)[27].

The point of emphasizing such variations is to show that, for the purposes of this chapter, it is necessary to understand the precise forms decentralisation takes in order to delineate its implications for teachers. It is safe to say that, for the most part, they add to the demands on and the responsibilities of the contemporary teacher, whether in terms of the organisation of learning, or concerning the deployment and management of resources in schools, or in responding to the exigencies of local and national accountability. As with the other areas discussed in this chapter, this can represent a very welcome enhancement of teacher professionalism and participation in educational organisation and decision-making. The CERI report summarises it thus in relation to decentralisation to the school level:

"... increased participation in decision-making reduces the sense of powerlessness and isolation experienced by many teachers as employees of a massive government bureaucracy. Participation in decision-making also develops an increased trust among participants in the administration of the school. This trust derives from the knowledge that structures and mechanisms now exist to reduce the possibility for excessive influence of a few. Teachers have access to information from sources other than the school leader. And, with an increase in the availability and flow of information, matters which irritated (such as concerns about inequitable allotments or assignments) explode less frequently. Moreover, as more staff become aware of the complexity of problems confronting the school administration, the "them versus us" mentality diminishes as well. School-based decision-making has encouraged and required teachers to address wider educational issues while interacting with teachers in other subject areas and grade levels, to address larger educational issues, to consider alternatives and to establish and defend positions" (p. 54)[27].

These different forms of change also rely on the "teacher factor" for their success. New responsibilities of leadership and liaison with communities, for principals and deputy principals especially, call for competences and professional approaches that need to be learned and tried, and they may make onerous demands on scarce time which may in turn suggest certain institutional reorganisation. Old habits and methods of work die hard; innovation and experimentation require a tolerant, even encouraging attitude from the responsible authorities and the community, not pressure to conform to the tried and tested. Account should be taken of the demands caused by significant change as a factor in its own right, in this case by decentralisation. And recognition is needed of the degree to which different forms of decentralisation assume for their success that teachers, individually and as members of corporate teams, are informed of developments and are up-to-date to a greater degree than hitherto. That in turn implies that learning and relearning are constant projects for teachers.

*
*   *

The discussion of each of the discrete new tasks and challenges illustrates a number of common themes. There is need for the proper assessment of the revision of teachers' practice, training, and the organisation of learning envisaged for the effective implementation of *any one* strategy, as well as the need to understand these in the light of the overall functioning of and demands on the school and the teacher, and the large and growing corresponding demand for teacher education, especially INSET. But no less important is what the different new strategies and demands add up to when taken altogether. The need for a comprehensive perspective must be underlined. That broad vision should encompass the implications for teacher time that all the tasks and strategies hold for the ability of teachers to fulfil their professional duties and to act as spearheads of educational improvement. Analysis of the time factor should be broadened to inform consideration of the appropriate organisational arrangements by which these new tasks and challenges are to be accommodated.

In all this, care must be taken to avoid placing too much faith in the capacity of teacher education and training as by themselves solutions for all current reforms and strategies. Attendance by the teacher on a course or seminars organised within a school, while essential, cannot alone ensure successful educational change and improvement. Ambitious but realistic appraisals are required, therefore, not only of the task of the modern teacher but of the potential of and capacity for teacher education. It is a necessary, certainly one of the most necessary, condition of successful change but it is not a sufficient one. The institutional and professional organisation of teaching, as well as the provision of appropriate support and facilities, are also vital.

The new tasks and challenges that enter the everyday practice of the modern teacher (and this chapter has presented but a selection) may be viewed from diametrically opposite perspectives: as additional burdens and cause for complaint or as elements of enhanced teacher expertise and professionalism. It is highly desirable, of course, that the latter should prevail. For this to occur, teachers will need to exercise a substantial degree of professional discretion and autonomy. This cannot take the form of purely individual initiatives, undertaken in the isolation of each class unit. Co-operation, co-ordination, and discussion are basic to the successful accomplishment of both the long-standing missions of education and to meeting the new tasks and challenges that now arise. Not only should this occur among teachers, but it also involves greater parental and community participation in education. Altogether, it means that teachers are expected not only to be responsible for good teaching, but increasingly are called upon to play their part in setting educational aims, keeping abreast, and resolving dilemmas and problems as they arise. In other words, the concept of "open professionalism" referred to in Chapter 3 remains just as valid for the 1990s as it was for the 1970s when it was developed.

NOTES AND REFERENCES

1. OECD (1985), "OECD Ministers discuss Education in Modern Society", Paris (the press communiqué issued 21 November, 1984), p. 46.
2. Lesourne, J. (1988), *L'éducation et la société de demain: à la recherche des vraies questions*, Ministère de l'Education Nationale, Editions La Découverte and *Journal Le Monde*, Paris, Chapter 15, "Les Enseignants". Chapter reproduced as "Les enseignants en France" (1988), (OECD working document in French only).
3. Department of Education and Science (England and Wales) (1983), *Teaching Quality*, HMSO, London.
4. Lawton, D. (1986), "The Role and Professional Status of the Teacher: Some Sociological Perspectives" (OECD working document), p. 2.
5. Lundgren, U. (1987), *New Challenges for Teachers and their Education,* Standing Conference of European Ministers of Education, Strasbourg.
6. For a good discussion of some of the long-term trends and changes that underpin education's place in society, see Coleman, J. and Husén, T. (1985), *Becoming Adult in a Changing Society*, OECD/CERI, Paris. A good discussion of the ways in which the modern teacher is in the midst of a variety of conflicting demands and pressures is Lundgren, U. (1987), *ibid.*
7. OECD (1990), *"Lone-Parent Families: The Economic Challenge*, Paris.
8. See Lawton, D. (1988), "Changes in Curriculum and Assessment: An Extended Role for the Teacher?" (OECD working document).
9. An in-depth presentation of the ramifications of curriculum reforms in Italy for teachers, both in terms of what is implied by the legislation (Laws 348 and 517) and what might secure their successful implementation is to be found in Ghilardi, F. (1988), "The Role of the Teacher in the light of Curriculum Reforms in Italian Schools: Legislation, Practice, and Some International Comparisons" (OECD working document).
10. As described in Lawton D. (1988), *op. cit.*, taking the example of England, the new General Certificate of Secondary Education (GCSE) which was introduced for the 16 year-old age group in 1986, and examined for the first time in 1988, included "empathy" as a small part of the new history syllabus. Before long, there was a public campaign denouncing teachers for departing from traditional views of what counts as history.
11. Jeffrey, A.W. (1985), "An International Study of the Core Skills Programme of the Youth Training Scheme for England and Wales: The Implications of the Core Skills and their Assessment in Scotland" (OECD working document).
12. A thorough review based on a series of national reports is to be found in Skilbeck, M. (1990), *Curriculum Reform: An Overview of Trends*, OECD/CERI, Paris.
13. Skilbeck, M. (1990), *ibid*, Chapters 4 and 6. See also OECD (1989), *Education and the Economy in a Changing Society*, Paris.
14. There is now a specific CERI activity on "Environment and School Initiatives".

15. A specific discussion of multiculturalism in relation to teachers and teacher training is contained in Abdallah-Pretceille, M. (1988), "Multicultural Policies and Consequences for Teachers" and "Multicultural Policies and Consequences for Teacher Education" (OECD working documents). See also OECD/CERI (1987), *Multicultural Education*, Paris.

16. For a discussion of trends and issues, with extensive statistics related to the formal education system of OECD countries, see OECD (1986), *Girls and Women in Education: A cross-national study of sex inequalities in upbringing and in schools and colleges*, Paris.

17. See Woolfson, R. (1987), "Integration of the Handicapped in Schools and its Implications for Teachers: Lessons from Research" (OECD working document). Initiatives in teacher training are discussed in Andrews, R.J. (1988), "Implications for Teacher Education of Students with Disabilities into Mainstream Schools" (OECD working document). More general enquiries into the movement towards integration are contained in OECD/CERI (1981), *The Education of the Handicapped – Integration in the School*, Paris, and (1985), *Integration of the Handicapped in Secondary Schools*, Paris.

18. Churchill, S. (1987), "Policy Development in Education in Multicultural Societies: Trends and Processes in the OECD countries", in OECD/CERI, *Multicultural Education, op. cit.*

19. Useful readers and summaries are Michel, A. (1986), *Down with Stereotypes! Eliminating Sexism from Children's Literature and School Textbooks*, UNESCO, Paris; Whyte, J., Deem, R., Kant, L. and Cruikshank, M. (eds.) (1985), *Girl-Friendly Schooling*, Methuen, London; Council of Europe (1982), *Sex Stereotyping in Schools* (A report of the Educational Workshop held in Honefoss, 5-8 May, 1981) Swets and Zeitlinger, Lisse.

20. For a useful discussion see IFAPLAN (1985), *Gender Equality Action Handbook*, Community Action Programme, Transition of Young People from Education to Adult and Working Life, Brussels.

21. Biklen, D.P. (1985), "Mainstreaming: From Compliance to Quality", *The Journal of Learning Disabilities*, Vol. 18.

22. See, for example, Leyser, Y. and Abrams, P.D. (1982), "Teacher Attitudes towards Normal and Exceptional Groups", *Journal of Psychology*, No. 110.

23. OECD/CERI (1986), *New Information Technologies: A Challenge for Education*, Paris.

24. SED/OECD (1988), *Microcomputers and Secondary Teaching: Implications for Teacher Education* (Report of an International Seminar arranged by the Scottish Education Department in co-operation with OECD, 12-15 October 1987), Glasgow; and OECD (1988), "The Use of Microcomputers in Education: Implications for Education" (OECD working document), Paris.

25. OECD/CERI (1987), *Information Technologies and Basic Learning: Reading, Writing, Science and Mathematics*, Paris.

26. OECD/CERI (1989), *Information Technologies in Education: The Quest for Quality Software*, Paris.

27. Examples taken from OECD/CERI (1989), "Decentralisation and School Improvement: New Perspectives and Conditions for Change" (OECD working document).

Chapter 6

THE TEACHER TODAY: AN OVERVIEW OF THE PROBLEM

TEACHERS IN THE SPOTLIGHT

In the large majority of OECD countries, teachers and teacher policies have become the centre of considerable concern and attention. The importance now being given to the improvement of the quality of education has no doubt been one major factor behind this. On the negative side, doubts are commonly expressed about the ability of new arrivals to the profession and their readiness for the rigours of the classroom. Critics question the capacity of the teaching force either to maintain established standards or to adapt to the modern world. The gradual ageing of the profession arouses worries about inadequate levels of "new blood" coming in. The more positive reason directly linking teachers to qualitative improvement is the growing awareness among policy-makers and the public at large that such improvement can only be achieved through, not in spite of, teachers. Educational reform, no matter how well designed in other respects, needs competent, motivated staff in classrooms and workshops to succeed. Meanwhile, there are signs of teacher shortages emerging on a worrying scale. These are most apparent in the very disciplines, such as mathematics and the sciences, different branches of technical and vocational education, and languages, that are currently accorded priority to realise the aims of economic adjustment and the promotion of international understanding. Shortages are closely related to the aims of raising quality of education; they threaten to undermine the capacity of education and training services, now and in the future, to deliver provision of the high quality universally expected of them.

The call for increased accountability is felt in education no less than in other policy spheres, another factor focusing attention on teachers. Parents are increasingly demanding in their desire for their children's success, and are more closely familiar with the educational world than ever before. The previously "closed world" of schools and classrooms is being gradually opened up. Questions are then asked about individual teachers and schools and, more generally, whether the profession as a whole provides value for the substantial public resources already devoted to it. That enquiry can only become still more intense if financial rewards are raised in the effort to improve the attractiveness of teaching to talented graduates and able practitioners.

Yet, while more accountability may be sought in order to impose limits on the freedom of action of teachers, the demands made on them imply that they should function autonomously and creatively, deploying a wide répertoire of advanced professional skills. The knowledge and attitudes of young people are shaped by media and peer-group influences often well beyond classroom control; nonetheless, scrutiny of learning outcomes is predominantly associated with the performance of teachers. Both are examples of the conflicting pressures they are subject to.

Teachers themselves often perceive another source of conflict to lie in the fact that their professional role is broadening at the same time as recognition and rewards tend to fall short of what they feel they deserve. The sense of dissatisfaction that this gives rise to can be counted as a further reason why teachers have moved into the spotlight of public concern. This dissatisfaction has been demonstrated most explicitly through damaging disputes over pay and conditions during the 1980s in settings as diverse as Greece, Ireland, Italy, New Zealand, Norway, Spain, Sweden, the United Kingdom, and some of the major city districts of the United States. Whether or not these have brought the social recognition that teachers so often complain is lacking, they have succeeded in attracting public attention.

CONDITIONS AND REWARDS

Though the most common picture is one of problematic status and rewards, the situation of teachers varies widely across OECD countries. In some, for instance, the profession still enjoys substantial prestige and competition for entry is keen (as in Japan). Their legal status differs – in some countries, especially those in continental Europe (such as Denmark, France, Germany, Greece, Italy, Luxembourg, Portugal, Spain) they are tenured civil servants. In nearly all countries, the pupil/teacher ratio has fallen steadily (even here there are exceptions), but, despite data deficiencies that preclude precise comparisons, it is also clear that actual magnitudes differ markedly from country to country.

The present inadequacies of international data on salaries and financial benefits make comparisons difficult in this domain, too. Studies have tended to confirm that there has been slippage in the financial rewards of teaching compared with competing occupations, as other sectors have enjoyed higher levels of salary growth and career increments in many countries. Although public-sector spending restraint limits the scope for significant salary increases in the short term, especially in view of the sheer size of the teaching profession, in some cases the relative decline has been reversed. In the United States, for instance, the average annual salaries of teachers in the public sector rose in constant dollars from $22 664 in 1980/81 to $26 551 by 1986/87. If teacher shortages threaten to become more widespread in the decade ahead, the authorities in those countries affected may face little option but to consider making teaching financially still more attractive. This concerns not only average levels of pay but also how salaries are distributed and structured over the career. How beneficial is it, for instance, for the able teacher to be rapidly rewarded with tangible pay increases if the maximum is soon attained and the only alternative for improvement is promotion out of the classroom? Yet starting salaries must also be set high enough to encourage young graduates to enter in the first place. A number of countries and authorities have also begun experimentation with different forms of financial incentives to target groups of practising and potential teachers.

Important though salaries undoubtedly are as an element of the profession's attractiveness, non-pecuniary conditions and rewards are crucial, too. Among these, the general isolation of teachers is a continuing source of strain and limits the range of professional response to educational challenges. Few, if any, other occupations place such faith in the organisational unit of the solitary professional. Nor is it well understood by people outside education how tiring teaching in front of a class actually is. A further general problem is that so long as teachers choose to follow their vocation and remain in the classroom, the actual nature of teaching changes little throughout the career even if new materials, tasks, and groups of students are added.

Extending career opportunities and stimulating diversity in the work are thus key elements in increasing both the attractiveness of the profession and the quality and flexibility of the education provided. They imply re-examination of the predominant practice whereby teachers continue to work full-time, full-year, up to a fixed retirement age. For experienced teachers, more flexible combinations of classroom teaching with other roles and duties, in schools and in enterprises and administrations outside, can yield substantial benefits and offer the additional boost to efficiency of reducing fatigue and "burn-out".

Extending career opportunities means not only to enhance diversity and interest for all teachers but also to improve promotion chances for one very important section of the profession – women. So important is the contribution that women make to the teaching service in all OECD countries that their situation cannot be regarded as a sectional concern. But so divergent are their career patterns and prospects from those of men that the special situation of female teachers should be addressed as a matter of urgency, for obvious reasons of equity but also with the view of ensuring that sufficient numbers of women continue to be attracted into teaching in the future. It is common across OECD countries for women to be seriously under-represented in promoted posts, especially principalships. While some countries report modest improvements in the proportions of female principals, in some the trend instead is for women to obtain even fewer such posts.

NEW CHALLENGES AND DEMANDS

In contemporary societies, schools and teachers are readily allotted a major role in contributing to the solution of an array of economic, social, and cultural problems that would have seemed quite foreign to their predecessors of decades gone by. The political pressure to quicken the pace of educational reform has inevitable consequences for the demands made on teachers. Alongside worries about salaries and insufficient social recognition, teachers are increasingly voicing concern about the sheer availability of time and about their preparedness as a body to do justice to these different challenges. It is in the interests of all that the extension of the teacher's role should constitute a source of professionalism based on expertise rather than be simply burdensome additions of ever greater numbers of new responsibilities. To achieve that may prove to be a sometimes painful process for all the parties concerned – from teachers, it will require acceptance that established practice may well be insufficient to meet contemporary demands; from parents and communities, the understanding that their own earlier experience of education will often fail to provide a reliable guide for what is best for the present young; from the authorities, full recognition of what is actually expected of teachers today in the fulfilment of their duties.

Few can doubt that the teacher's task has become more demanding in recent times. In a number of countries, for example, teachers have acquired responsibilities for designing and implementing curriculum reform and for introducing new forms of student assessment. These call on a wider répertoire of skills, and more active co-operation by teachers with their colleagues, parents, and other bodies in the community. Current policy priorities call for "horizontal" strategies that depend on teachers for their success. One is the general expectation that teachers impart an understanding of, and positive attitudes towards, the worlds of employment and work, giving guidance to their students as appropriate. Knowledge and understanding of other countries has now to be promoted by teachers, schools and colleges as part of efforts to foster "internationalisation". This is not new but it takes on fresh significance in the light of the rapidity of recent international developments and the growing interdependence in the world economy. Targeted programmes – such as multiculturalism, equality of the sexes, and the integration of disabled pupils into mainstream schools – all represent far-reaching areas of reform where the teacher's role is pivotal. The successful introduction of information technology into classrooms depends on their informed and imaginative application by teachers. And new moral and social questions are being added to their brief: to enhance awareness of the environment and pollution, to educate about drug abuse and AIDS, to be watchful for signs of child abuse in the home.

Each of these demands alone implies ambitious programmes of pre- and in-service teacher education and the reorganisation of learning. From the standpoint of the classroom teacher and school principal, what matters is that they are expected to promote these strategies actively, and all at once. This challenge calls for comprehensive vision. The preservice phase of teacher education must accommodate these diverse competing developments in ways that do not jeopardize its practical usefulness to prepare for entry into the profession nor dilute the quality of the programmes. It should be decided what best be taken up instead through continuing in-service education and training and whether current opportunities for these are adequate to keep the profession informed and abreast of new developments. And changes that are at present introduced discretely and piecemeal may call for the comprehensive review of institutional structures and classroom organisation, taking account of teachers' duties – individually and collectively – in their entirety.

SIGNS OF SHORTAGE

The emerging issue of teacher shortages has already been mentioned as a major factor causing the spotlight to fall on teachers. Not all countries are currently reporting general shortages and in one or two cases, such as Germany and Ireland, surplus remains, for the present at least, the immediate concern. But all OECD countries are experiencing some shortfall in certain disciplines and in specific regions, whether these are inner-city districts or isolated rural communities or areas of high-cost housing, or as manifested through the continued deployment of unqualified staff. And all countries might well expect to be affected, to varying degrees, by trends already visible that threaten to exacerbate shortages over the decade. Four of these trends stand out.

The first is the "greying" of the teaching profession – the consequence of the major recruitment drives of the late 1950s and 60s followed by severe curtailment of intake from the mid-1970s (the timing differs by country) – that will inevitably result in quickening losses through retirement. Simply replacing these will call for new recruitment drives. Meanwhile, many OECD countries struggle with the legacy of years of lean recruitment which substantially reduced initial training capacity and solidified the image of a profession that offers few openings.

Second, the complex interplay between student demand for education and training and demographic trends continues to pose major difficulties for matching teacher supply and demand and renders long-term planning extremely hazardous. The common pattern is of falling student rolls in lower secondary schools which contrast with a partial revival of numbers at the primary level following a rise in numbers of births in some countries, and a still growing demand for pre-primary education from working parents in many of them. Larger numbers of students may well stay in upper secondary education and training through the 1990s, directly encouraged by public policy. In France, for example, the ambitious official target is approximately to double the proportion of youngsters who achieve the *baccalauréat* qualification to attain 8 in 10 by the year 2000. Against this can be set the smaller cohorts passing through the higher education systems from which new entrants to teaching are mainly drawn.

Third, for the years ahead the labour market will almost inevitably be characterised by sharpened general competition and shortages in activities that require advanced skills – which is likely to leave teaching at an even bigger disadvantage in its efforts to attract talented graduates. The availability of more lucrative openings in industry and commerce is a matter of concern not only to education authorities; it affects equally other types of service employment that have traditionally relied on substantial inflows of young adults, such as the health sector and military services. Teaching must be a profession attractive enough, therefore, to compete with all these sectors.

Fourth, the changing labour-market behaviour and experiences of women could well mean that they become a less reliable source of supply of new or returning teachers than they have proved hitherto. As their work aspirations and behaviour come more closely to resemble those of men, women might be expected to share more closely with them a negative assessment of the career potential of teaching. Women should thus constitute an important focus of policies to combat teacher shortages. One aspect of this has been discussed already: the need to address current opportunities for and practices towards promotion. Others might include the targeting of recruitment drives and special incentives policies towards women. Such a focus might also usefully involve addressing the facilities and benefits for teachers with onerous family responsibilities.

Given the need to combat teacher shortages, especially as these affect the disciplinary areas of mathematics and sciences and technical and vocational education, efforts to encourage entrants to teaching from other occupational backgrounds could well pay substantial dividends. Pre- and in-service education programmes need to be designed to give such teachers sound preparation for the classroom and to ensure that teaching standards are not relaxed in the face of the desire to boost numbers. Proper induction and follow-up support – essential for all new teachers – are an important component of the preparation needed for those teachers entering through the less orthodox routes. Serious attention might also be given to higher education programmes and qualifications – whether mainly for teaching or other fields – characterised by "polyvalence", aiming to permit a greater degree of mobility in and out of the profession. Promoting greater diversity of entry, and of types of careers within teaching once entered, may well prove beneficial not only in alleviating shortages but in enhancing the attractiveness of the profession, the familiarity of teachers with outside developments and occupations, and the very quality of the education provided. It should not conflict, however, with the aim of developing clearer career structures for those following more orthodox patterns.

MAINTAINING TEACHER QUALITY: SELECTION, PREPARATION, AND APPRAISAL

The question of the quality of new recruits and practising teachers is inextricably related to all the matters – conditions and rewards, new tasks and challenges, meeting shortages – dealt with above. In particular, teacher supply and demand cannot be regarded as a predominantly quantitative matter; the aim must be to maintain an adequate supply of *high quality* teachers, professionally competent and temperamentally suited to classroom life.

Often, public discussion of teacher quality is preoccupied with the academic abilities of the student intake to pre-service courses and of new entrants. Doubts are commonly expressed. The professional demands of teaching today do indeed suggest the need for teachers to be intellectually able; competent in their field and able to keep abreast of new developments, and capable of applying their knowledge and skills to new situations as the need arises.

But the preoccupation with the academic backgrounds of new entrants provides only a limited perspective on the ingredients of teacher quality. The contrast frequently drawn, for instance, between the need for teachers to possess sound academic credentials *versus* good practical preparation for classrooms and workshops is a false one. Teachers should possess mastery of subject matter *and* be able to transmit that successfully to the students in their charge. Pedagogical skills, educational understanding, and an appropriate personality for teaching are all contributing factors. Equally, concerning teacher education, attention to the academic prowess of the student intake has often been to the relative neglect of the quality of the programmes and staff actually providing it. Several OECD countries are now seeking to redress that balance. Teacher selection concerns the adequacy and preparedness of those *conducting* the selection no less than the qualities sought after in those *being selected*. The same applies with promotion and appraisal. And the quality of staff is not something established and fixed from the outset as reflected by early grades in college; it is to be nurtured through in-service education and training and career development.

The question of teacher assessment and appraisal is a controversial one in many countries. Conflicting arguments circulate about whether they foster or limit professionalism, about their aims in terms of professional development or reward, and about the feasibility of different schemes. It is a corollary of the sheer diversity of the ingredients of teacher professionalism and good teaching, that the *comprehensive* assessment of each individual's work is an especially challenging, and potentially costly, undertaking. But it should also be recognised that a considerable amount of evaluation of teachers' work is already normal practice, whether that concerns the suitability of students for teaching, their performance as probationers, the achievements of each teacher within school departments, or selection for promoted posts. The issue is not so much whether there should be assessment of professional performance but its nature, who is responsible for it, and how it is to be used. The scope of assessment and appraisal is thus broad, extending well beyond the much-discussed problem of identifying the patently weak teacher. For this small minority who are clearly inadequate, there should be mechanisms, in the interests of their colleagues and the pupils in their charge, whereby they are reassigned out of the classroom or out of education altogether, if reasonable efforts at retraining fail.

INFORMATION AND RESEARCH: QUESTIONS ON THE AGENDA

The potential research agenda deriving only from this OECD report, quite apart from the myriad other commentaries and studies on teachers and teacher policies across the different countries, is an endless one. Nevertheless, there are certain areas that emerge as especially deserving of sustained enquiry either because current information is patently deficient or because of the importance to the educational enterprise of improved knowledge and understanding in those fields.

Nationally and for the purposes of international comparisons, there are substantial deficiencies in the basic statistical information available on teacher numbers and their distribution. Even for a single recent year, it is extremely difficult to arrive at a comprehensive picture of teacher numbers across OECD countries as a whole, following agreed classifications of the personnel included and hours worked in terms of full-time equivalence. Detailed information is lacking for many countries concerning the meaning and incidence of part-time and relief teaching. The deficiencies are compounded when the aim is to calculate and compare pupil/teacher ratios (PTRs) or to delineate trends in these different areas across time. Improvements can be sought in both national data and in the co-ordination and calculation of statistics and indicators cross-nationally.

The growing importance of the complex issues surrounding teacher supply, surplus, and shortage call for very sound information to inform debate. One useful classification of teacher shortages is:

- *overt* shortage: the obvious case of continued unfilled vacancies;
- *hidden* shortage: teaching provided by the inappropriately qualified or the unqualified;
- *suppressed* shortage: amendment of and distortion to the curriculum through lack of suitable staff.

Information on these categories can usefully be supplemented by the reliable documentation of such matters as teachers' rates of leaving and to which destinations, and on their attitudes towards work and career. Analyses of possible medium- and long-term developments should seek to avoid the shortcomings of rigid forecasting exercises. One profitable way forward could well prove to be the elaboration of *alternative* scenarios for teacher supply and demand using differing assumptions concerning the magnitudes of predictive variables. The power of the analysis would then lie in the elaboration of the implications for teacher demand of differing assumptions, rather than the generation of single predictions.

Comparisons of teachers' rewards and benefits are fraught with problems concerning the differing treatment on such matters as housing and mobility allowances, social security and pension rights, payment during holidays, as well as salary and incentive structures themselves. If comparisons are to be meaningfully conducted in the area of teacher rewards – with other occupations, over time, across countries – further clarification of these components and consolidation of data are required.

Many countries have recently introduced schemes, innovations, and experiments in a variety of fields aiming to enhance the attractiveness of the profession to all and to target groups of teachers, or seeking to increase and/or diversify recruitment. Some are directed at students considering a course of study and career, others at practising teachers. They include such schemes as new student aid packages, information campaigns, incentive allowances, revised fringe benefits, "merit pay", alternative channels of recruitment, job-sharing arrangements, and school/industry linking projects. There are also new policies for teacher appraisal in a number of countries. Some evaluation is already underway on these; they could usefully be the subject of more extensive review and international exchange. Apart from simply describing such programmes and their scale, the search should be to identify both good practice and experienced shortcomings.

There are a number of different categories of teaching staff whose particular situation and problems arguably deserve special scrutiny. Such a list might include those in pre-primary institutions, beginning teachers in induction and the early years, staff from alternative occupational backgrounds, those in shortage subjects. One section of the teaching force that tends often to be neglected in mainstream discussion are those in the vocational and technical fields. That sector has acquired particular importance over recent years with a major responsibility for the youngsters encouraged to remain in education and training, and nowhere are the pressures keener for staff to remain abreast of outside developments. Existing gulfs between the cultures of "education" and "training" are likely to prove highly counterproductive to students, teachers, and to the provision of learning opportunities adaptable to the needs of all. The question of the sources of recruitment and methods of training for the teachers in vocational education in order to provide high-quality and flexible programmes is thus a matter deserving further attention.

Research into teaching itself, linked practically, as far as possible, to the concrete tasks of the classroom teacher, should continue to be a high priority. Our understanding of what makes for effective learning, teacher competence, and for worthwhile approaches to teaching and to organising classrooms generally, has grown substantially over recent years. The particular requirements of teaching special populations have been increasingly studied. The pedagogical, organisational, and teacher education and training implications of the research should, in particular, be further developed, informed by a wholistic understanding of teachers' work.

THE SEARCH FOR CONSENSUS

In the light of the difficulties experienced in a number of countries in recent years, difficulties that have proved counterproductive to educational progress, there is the need for the active pursuit of greater consensus among all concerned. A groundswell of optimism and public recognition for the difficult and demanding task that teachers perform can potentially reap ready rewards in the form of boosted morale, enhanced motivation, and the greater attractiveness of the profession that can become self-generating, with obviously positive results for teaching and learning. Distrust, confrontation, and mutual suspicion between the different parties involved result ultimately in dented morale and a decline of teaching standards. That is a vicious circle that modern societies and economies can ill afford. To win that recognition and support, it is only reasonable that the highest standards of professional performance and commitment are to be expected from all teachers in return.

WHERE TO OBTAIN OECD PUBLICATIONS
OÙ OBTENIR LES PUBLICATIONS DE L'OCDE

Argentina – Argentine
Carlos Hirsch S.R.L.
Galería Güemes, Florida 165, 4° Piso
1333 Buenos Aires   Tel. 30.7122, 331.1787 y 331.2391
Telegram: Hirsch–Baires
Telex: 21112 UAPE–AR. Ref. s/2901
Telefax:(1)331–1787

Australia – Australie
D.A. Book (Aust.) Pty. Ltd.
648 Whitehorse Road, P.O.B 163
Mitcham, Victoria 3132   Tel. (03)873.4411
Telex: AA37911 DA BOOK
Telefax: (03)873.5679

Austria – Autriche
OECD Publications and Information Centre
4 Simrockstrasse
5300 Bonn (Germany)   Tel. (0228)21.60.45
Telex: 8 86300 Bonn
Telefax: (0228)26.11.04

Gerold & Co.
Graben 31
Wien I   Tel. (0222)533.50.14

Belgium – Belgique
Jean De Lannoy
Avenue du Roi 202
B–1060 Bruxelles   Tel. (02)538.51.69/538.08.41
Telex: 63220   Telefax: (02) 538.08.41

Canada
Renouf Publishing Company Ltd.
1294 Algoma Road
Ottawa, ON K1B 3W8   Tel. (613)741.4333
Telex: 053–4783   Telefax: (613)741.5439
Stores:
61 Sparks Street
Ottawa, ON K1P 5R1   Tel. (613)238.8985
211 Yonge Street
Toronto, ON M5B 1M4   Tel. (416)363.3171

Federal Publications
165 University Avenue
Toronto, ON M5H 3B9   Tel. (416)581.1552
Telefax: (416)581.1743

Les Publications Fédérales
1185 rue de l'Université
Montréal, PQ H3B 3A7   Tel.(514)954–1633

Les Éditions La Liberté Inc.
3020 Chemin Sainte–Foy
Sainte–Foy, PQ G1X 3V6   Tel. (418)658.3763
    Telefax: (418)658.3763

Denmark – Danemark
Munksgaard Export and Subscription Service
35, Norre Sogade, P.O. Box 2148
DK–1016 København K   Tel. (45 33)12.85.70
Telex: 19431 MUNKS DK   Telefax: (45 33)12.93.87

Finland – Finlande
Akateeminen Kirjakauppa
Keskuskatu 1, P.O. Box 128
00100 Helsinki   Tel. (358 0)12141
Telex: 125080   Telefax: (358 0)121.4441

France
OECD/OCDE
Mail Orders/Commandes par correspondance:
2 rue André–Pascal
75775 Paris Cedex 16   Tel. (1)45.24.82.00
Bookshop/Librairie:
33, rue Octave–Feuillet
75016 Paris   Tel. (1)45.24.81.67
    (1)45.24.81.81
Telex: 620 160 OCDE
Telefax: (33–1)45.24.85.00

Librairie de l'Université
12a, rue Nazareth
13602 Aix–en–Provence   Tel. 42.26.18.08

Germany – Allemagne
OECD Publications and Information Centre
4 Simrockstrasse
5300 Bonn   Tel. (0228)21.60.45
Telex: 8 86300 Bonn   Telefax: (0228)26.11.04

Greece – Grèce
Librairie Kauffmann
28 rue du Stade
105 64 Athens   Tel. 322.21.60
Telex: 218187 LIKA Gr

Hong Kong
Swindon Book Co. Ltd.
13 – 15 Lock Road
Kowloon, Hongkong   Tel. 366 80 31
Telex: 50 441 SWIN HX
Telefax: 739 49 75

Iceland – Islande
Mál Mog Menning
Laugavegi 18, Pósthólf 392
121 Reykjavik   Tel. 15199/24240

India – Inde
Oxford Book and Stationery Co.
Scindia House
New Delhi 110001   Tel. 331.5896/5308
Telex: 31 61990 AM IN
Telefax: (11)332.5993
17 Park Street
Calcutta 700016   Tel. 240832

Indonesia – Indonésie
Pdii–Lipi
P.O. Box 269/JKSMG/88
Jakarta 12790   Tel. 583467
Telex: 62 875

Ireland – Irlande
TDC Publishers – Library Suppliers
12 North Frederick Street
Dublin 1   Tel. 744835/749677
Telex: 33530 TDCP EI Telefax : 748416

Italy – Italie
Libreria Commissionaria Sansoni
Via Benedetto Fortini, 120/10
Casella Post. 552
50125 Firenze   Tel. (055)645415
Telex: 570466   Telefax: (39.55)641257
Via Bartolini 29
20155 Milano   Tel. 365083
La diffusione delle pubblicazioni OCSE viene assicurata dalle
principali librerie ed anche da:
Editrice e Libreria Herder
Piazza Montecitorio 120
00186 Roma   Tel. 679.4628
Telex: NATEL I 621427
Libreria Hoepli
Via Hoepli 5
20121 Milano   Tel. 865446
Telex: 31.33.95 Telefax: (39.2)805.2886
Libreria Scientifica
Dott. Lucio de Biasio "Aeiou"
Via Meravigli 16
20123 Milano   Tel. 807679
Telefax: 800175

Japan– Japon
OECD Publications and Information Centre
Landic Akasaka Building
2–3–4 Akasaka, Minato–ku
Tokyo 107   Tel. 586.2016
Telefax: (81.3)584.7929

Korea – Corée
Kyobo Book Centre Co. Ltd.
P.O. Box 1658, Kwang Hwa Moon
Seoul   Tel. (REP)730.78.91
Telefax: 735.0030

**Malaysia/Singapore –
Malaisie/Singapour**
University of Malaya Co–operative Bookshop Ltd.
P.O. Box 1127, Jalan Pantai Baru 59100
Kuala Lumpur
Malaysia   Tel. 756.5000/756.5425
Telefax: 757.3661

Information Publications Pte. Ltd.
Pei–Fu Industrial Building
24 New Industrial Road No. 02–06
Singapore 1953   Tel. 283.1786/283.1798
Telefax: 284.8875

Netherlands – Pays–Bas
SDU Uitgeverij
Christoffel Plantijnstraat 2
Postbus 20014
2500 EA's–Gravenhage   Tel. (070 3)78.99.11
Voor bestellingen: Tel. (070 3)78.98.80
Telex: 32486 stdru   Telefax: (070 3)47.63.51

New Zealand – Nouvelle–Zélande
Government Printing Office
Customer Services
P.O. Box 12–411
Freepost 10–050
Thorndon, Wellington
Tel. 0800 733–406   Telefax: 04 499–1733

Norway – Norvège
Narvesen Info Center – NIC
Bertrand Narvesens vei 2
P.O. Box 6125 Etterstad
0602 Oslo 6   Tel. (02)57.33.00
Telex: 79668 NIC N   Telefax: (02)68.19.01

Pakistan
Mirza Book Agency
65 Shahrah Quaid–E–Azam
Lahore 3   Tel. 66839
Telex: 44886 UBL PK. Attn: MIRZA BK

Portugal
Livraria Portugal
Rua do Carmo 70–74
Apart. 2681
1117 Lisboa Codex   Tel. 347.49.82/3/4/5

**Singapore/Malaysia
Singapour/Malaisie**
See "Malaysia/Singapore"
Voir "Malaisie/Singapour"

Spain – Espagne
Mundi–Prensa Libros S.A.
Castelló 37, Apartado 1223
Madrid 28001   Tel. (91) 431.33.99
Telex: 49370 MPLI   Telefax: 575 39 98
Libreria Internacional AEDOS
Consejo de Ciento 391
08009 –Barcelona   Tel. (93) 301–86–15
Telefax: (93) 317–01–41

Sweden – Suède
Fritzes Fackboksföretaget
Box 16356, S 103 27 STH
Regeringsgatan 12
DS Stockholm   Tel. (08)23.89.00
Telex: 12387 Telefax: (08)20.50.21
Subscription Agency/Abonnements:
Wennergren–Williams AB
Box 30004
104 25 Stockholm   Tel. (08)54.12.00
Telex: 19937 Telefax: (08)50.82.86

Switzerland – Suisse
OECD Publications and Information Centre
4 Simrockstrasse
5300 Bonn (Germany)   Tel. (0228)21.60.45
Telex: 8 86300 Bonn
Telefax: (0228)26.11.04

Librairie Payot
6 rue Grenus
1211 Genève 11   Tel. (022)731.89.50
Telex: 28356
Maditec S.A.
Ch. des Palettes 4
1020 Renens/Lausanne   Tel. (021)635.08.65
Telefax: (021)635.07.80
United Nations Bookshop/Librairie des Nations–Unies
Palais des Nations
1211 Genève 10   Tel. (022)734.60.11 (ext. 48.72)
Telex: 289696 (Attn: Sales)
Telefax: (022)733.98.79

Taiwan – Formose
Good Faith Worldwide Int'l. Co. Ltd.
9th Floor, No. 118, Sec. 2
Chung Hsiao E. Road
Taipei   Tel. 391.7396/391.7397
Telefax: (02) 394.9176

Thailand – Thaïlande
Suksit Siam Co. Ltd.
1715 Rama IV Road, Samyan
Bangkok 5   Tel. 251.1630

Turkey – Turquie
Kültur Yayinlari Is–Türk Ltd. Sti.
Atatürk Bulvari No. 191/Kat. 21
Kavaklidere/Ankara   Tel. 25.07.60
Dolmabahce Cad. No. 29
Besiktas/Istanbul   Tel. 160.71.88
Telex: 43482B

United Kingdom – Royaume–Uni
HMSO
Gen. enquiries   Tel. (071) 873 0011
Postal orders only:
P.O. Box 276, London SW8 5DT
Personal Callers HMSO Bookshop
49 High Holborn, London WC1V 6HB
Telex: 297138 Telefax: 071 873 8463
Branches at: Belfast, Birmingham, Bristol, Edinburgh,
Manchester

United States – États–Unis
OECD Publications and Information Centre
2001 L Street N.W., Suite 700
Washington, D.C. 20036–4095   Tel. (202)785.6323
Telefax: (202)785.0350

Venezuela
Libreria del Este
Avda F. Miranda 52, Aptdo. 60337
Edificio Galipán
Caracas 106   Tel. 951.1705/951.2307/951.1297
Telegram: Libreste Caracas

Yugoslavia – Yougoslavie
Jugoslovenska Knjiga
Knez Mihajlova 2, P.O. Box 36
Beograd   Tel. 621.992
Telex: 12466 jk bgd

Orders and inquiries from countries where Distributors have
not yet been appointed should be sent to: OECD Publications
Service, 2 rue André–Pascal, 75775 Paris Cedex 16, France.
Les commandes provenant de pays où l'OCDE n'a pas encore
désigné de distributeur devraient être adressées à : OCDE,
Service des Publications, 2, rue André–Pascal, 75775 Paris
Cedex 16, France.

8/90

OECD PUBLICATIONS, 2 rue André-Pascal, 75775 PARIS CEDEX 16
PRINTED IN FRANCE
(91 90 03 1) ISBN 92-64-13413-1 - No. 45313 1990